The  100 Best Walks in
Heart of England

Produced by AA Publishing
© Automobile Association Developments
Limited 2004
Reprinted 2005
Reprinted 2007

Published by AA Publishing (a trading name
of Automobile Association Developments
Limited, whose registered office is Fanum
House, Basing View, Basingstoke,
Hampshire RG21 4EA; registered number
1878835)

 This product includes
mapping data licensed
from Ordnance Survey® with the permission
of the Controller of Her Majesty's Stationery
Office.
© Crown copyright 2007. All rights reserved.
Licence number 100021153

ISBN-10: 0-7495-4049-4
ISBN-13: 978-0-7495-4049-4
A03364

Please write to:
AA Publishing, FH13, Fanum House,
Basing View, Basingstoke RG21 4EA

These routes appear in the *AA Local Walks*
series and *1001 Walks in Britain*.

Visit AA Publishing at:
www.theAA.com/travel

Colour reproduction by:
Keene Group, Andover
Printed and bound by:
Oriental Press, Dubai

Acknowledgements

Written and researched by Christopher
Knowles, Nicholas Reynolds, David
Hancock, Ann F Stonehouse, Julie Royle,
Nick Channer, Roger Noyce, Paul Grogan,
Moira McCrossan and Hugh Taylor

Picture credits

All images are held in the Automobile
Association's own photo library (AA World
Travel Library) and were taken by the
following photographers:
Front cover AA; 3 A Tryner;
4/5 A J Hopkins; 6/7 M Birkitt;
8/9 J Beazley; 10tr C Jones; 11cc S Day;
11cr S Day; 11br M Short; 12tl K Doran;
12tc M Short; 12tr A J Hopkins; 13 P Baker.

*Opposite: The church at Ilam Hall,
Staffordshire
Page 4: The tilted ridge of The
Roaches with Hen Cloud behind,
Staffordshire*

Contents

*Warwick Castle on the banks of
the River Avon, Warwickshire*

Heart of England

This is Shakespeare country, land of Oxford's dreaming spires, warm Cotswold stone and fine cathedral cities. Staffordshire claws its way into the Peak District, while Shropshire throws up hills on the Welsh border.

Walking near Hollinsclough in the Peak District

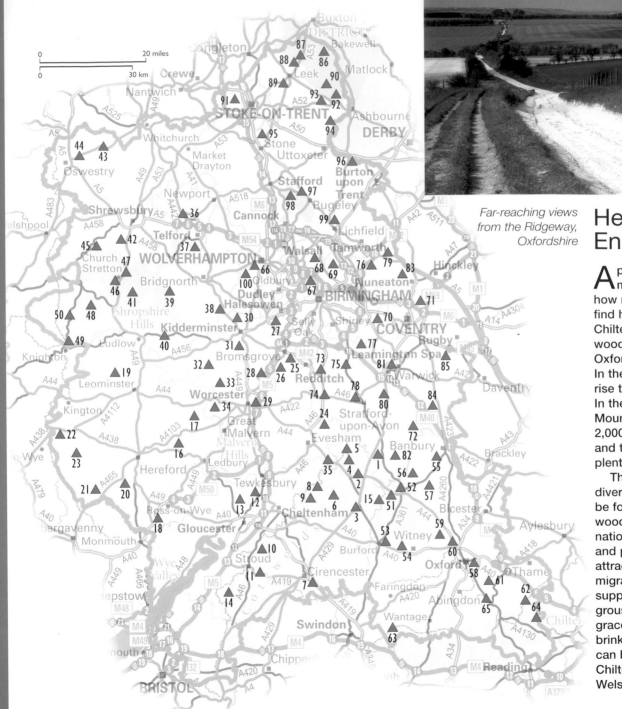

Far-reaching views from the Ridgeway, Oxfordshire

Heart of England

Apart from the canals, you may be surprised at just how much hill-country you'll find here. In the east the Chilterns form a natural beech-wooded boundary to Oxfordshire's farming country. In the middle the Cotswolds rise to a fine escarpment ridge. In the west the Black Mountains carry summits over 2,000ft (610m), and the Wrekin and the Shropshire Hills secure plenty of upland heritage.

There is a surprising diversity of natural habitats to be found here, from ancient woodlands, scrub and heath, to nationally important wetlands and peat bogs. Reservoirs attract a huge number of migrating birds and the moors support stonechat, buzzard, grouse and skylark. The graceful red kite, once on the brink of extinction in Britain, can be seen again over the Chilterns and the hills on the Welsh border.

The Black Country

The region can claim, with some justification, to have been the birthplace of the Industrial Revolution. In Shropshire Abraham Darby perfected his method of making iron in a blast furnace powered by coke. The new process meant that coal replaced wood as the vital raw material, along with limestone, which was crucial as a flux. The West Midlands were rich in both and canal pioneer James Brindley built a transport infrastructure to move the manufactured products to new markets. And at the heart of the new canal network stood Birmingham.

The Cotswolds

Perhaps the area of central England most visited by tourists is the triangle between the Cotswolds, Stratford-upon-Avon and Oxford. For most the attractions here are the buildings and the famous folk who lived in them. The shadow of William Shakespeare is everywhere in southern Warwickshire – every pub the bard drank in, every house where he stayed the night, claims to be some part of this literary giant's heritage. From here it is only a short drive into the Cotswolds and its villages of honey-coloured stone. Bourton-on-the-Water with its pretty bridges, Blockley, where former workers' cottages are now the epitome of Cotswold charm.

Top: The Cotswold villages of Blockley and Bourton-on-the-Water Right: Uffington, Oxfordshire

Towns too form an important aspect of walking in central England – Hereford, Worcester, Lichfield, Stourport, Bridgnorth and Droitwich are all worth exploring.

Canals and National Reserves

The dense network of canals, lined by peaceful tow paths, means that even central Birmingham can be a fine place to walk. Moreover, not all the canals in the region have survived the financial rigours of the last 200 years and their abandoned courses often become valuable wetland habitats. You'll find stretches of the Hereford and Gloucester at Ashperton, and the Thames and Severn at Chalford. Leisure craft are now the most important users on the canals today and the tow path provides an antidote to the car-choked roads of the Midlands. Tittesworth Reservoir in Staffordshire is a nationally important site for otters and water voles. Sutton Park, hemmed in by urban sprawl, is surely the least likely National Nature Reserve. Wetlands were once common throughout the region and you'll find the glacial meres of the 'Shropshire Lake District' around Ellesmere.

Above: Hotel sign in Stratford
Right: Part of Uffington's white
horse carved into the hillside

Royal Influence

Royalty has left its mark on the region. Oxford was Charles I's capital during the Civil War and we have included a walk around the city. The beer in Berkswell attracted Cromwell's soldiers to billet themselves in the local pubs, and perhaps the prospect of it that caused so many deserters on either side during that war's first major encounter. You can look over their battle site while walking along the Edge Hill escarpment at Ratley. Watlington battlefield is also included here, and there are sad memorials to other conflicts to be discovered on Cannock Chase and at Hanbury, where you'll find the crater left by the largest wartime explosion in history.

Literary Rambles

This is also Shakespeare Country. You can walk in the footsteps of the Bard around his Stratford-upon-Avon home, and you can see where he was allegedly arrested for poaching deer, at Charlecote. Shakespeare was not the only literary giant to draw inspiration from the area. The Slad Valley was Laurie Lee's childhood home and the subject of *Cider with Rosie*, while Ellastone in Staffordshire was the setting for George Elliott's *Adam Bede*. Writers flocked to the Garsington home of Lady Ottoline Morrell – a young Aldous Huxley, Bertrand Russel and many of that Bloomsbury set of literary and artistic radicals. However grand their ideas, though, none of them had as much impact on the world stage as another one-time Oxfordshire resident – Winston Churchill. You can see his birthplace at the extravagant Blenheim Palace, and see his grave at Bladon.

View from a Hill

Many walkers will want a simple hill to climb and the wind in their hair. Abdon Burf on Brown Clee is among the highest vantage points, at 1,770ft (540m), but there are other favourites. Mow Cop offers views across the Cheshire Plain and Staffordshire. The Stiperstones and the Long Mynd are perhaps Shropshire's best-known wild country, but Wenlock Edge and the shapely Strettons can hold their own. Staffordshire can claim some Pennine grit – venture out around the Roaches and you will suspect

The craggy tops of The Roaches in the Peak District

you are in the wrong region. Oxfordshire has a foothold in the Chilterns and on the Wessex Downs, where the White Horse of Uffington has been presiding over an airy prospect for over 3,000 years. Warwickshire's uplands are perhaps the least of all, but the view from the Dasset Hills is still a fine one.

Using this Book

❶ Information panels
Information panels show the total distance and total amount of ascent (that is how much ascent you will accumulate throughout the walk). An indication of the gradient you will

Cannock Chase, Staffordshire

encounter is shown by the rating 0–3. Zero indicates fairly flat ground and 3 indicates undulating terrain with several very steep slopes.

❷ Minimum time
The minimum time suggested is for approximate guidance only. It assumes reasonably fit walkers and doesn't allow for stops.

❸ Start points
The start of each walk is given as a six-figure grid reference prefixed by two letters indicating which 100km square of the National Grid it refers to. You'll find more information on grid references on most Ordnance Survey maps.

❹ Abbreviations
Walk directions use these abbreviations:
L – left
L–H – left-hand
R – right
R–H – right-hand
Names which appear on signposts are given in brackets, for example ('Bantam Beach').

❺ Suggested maps
Details of appropriate maps are given for each walk, and usually refer to 1:25,000 scale Ordnance Survey Explorer maps. We strongly recommend that you always take the appropriate OS map with you. Our hand-drawn maps are there to give you the route and do not show all the details or relief that you will need to navigate around the routes provided in this collection. You can purchase OS maps at all good bookshops, or by calling Stanfords on 020 7836 2260.

❻ Car parking
Many of the car parks suggested are public, but occasionally you may find you have to park on the roadside or in a lay-by. Please be considerate when you leave your car, ensuring that access roads or gates are not blocked and that other vehicles can pass safely. Remember that pub car parks are private and should not be used unless you are visiting the pub or you have the landlord's permission to park there.

---

00 Location Walk title

❶ 4½ miles (7.2km) 1hr 45min **Ascent:** 131ft (40m) ▲
Paths: Cliff top, shingle beach, farm track and country lanes, 1 stile
Suggested map: OS Explorer 231 Southwold & Bungay ❺
❸ **Grid reference:** TM 522818
Parking: On street near Covehithe church ❻

Country • Region

See the effects of coastal erosion on a walk along a rapidly disappearing cliff top.
❶ Take tarmac lane from **St Andrew's Church** down towards sea to barrier ('Danger') and sign warning that there is no public right of way. Although this is strictly true, this is well-established and popular path stretching north towards Kessingland beach and you are likely to meet many other walkers. The warnings are serious but it is quite safe to walk here so long as you keep away from the cliff edge.
❷ Walk through gap to **R** of road barrier and continue towards cliffs. Turn **L** along wide farm track with pig farm to your **L**. Path follows cliff top then descends towards beach to enter **Benacre nature reserve**. On **L** is **Benacre Broad**, once an estuary, now a marshy lagoon. The shingle beach attracts little terns in spring and summer and you should keep to the path to avoid their nesting sites.
❸ Climb back on to cliffs at end of Benacre Broad. The way cuts through pine trees and bracken on

constantly changing path before running alongside field and swinging **R** to descend to beach level, where you take wide grass track on your **L** across dunes.
❹ At concrete track, with tower of Kessingland church in distance, turn **L** following waymarks of **Suffolk Coast and Heaths Path**. Cross stile and keep straight ahead, passing **Beach Farm** on **R**. Stay straight ahead for 1 mile (1.6km) on wide track between fields with views of Benacre church ahead.
❺ Go through white gates and turn **L** on to quiet country lane. Stay on lane for ¾ mile (1.2km) as it passes between hedges with arable farmland to either side and swings **L** at entrance to **Hall Farm**.
❻ When road bends **R**, turn **L** past gate with an English Nature 'No Entry' sign for cars. Stay on this permissive path as it swings **R** around meadow and continues into woodland of **Holly Grove**. Pass through another gate and turn **L** along road for ¾ mile (1.2km) back into **Covehithe**. Turn **L** at junction to return to **St Andrew's Church**. ❹

Map legend

←	Walk route	P	Car park
•••	Optional walk route		Cliff
– – –	Adjoining footpath		Rock outcrop
–·–·–	County boundary		Beach
☼	Viewpoint		Woodland
▲ 392	Spot height		Parkland
	Built-up area	†	Church, cathedral, chapel
●	Place of interest	WC	Toilet
△	Steep section	⊞	Picnic area

1 The Ditchfords The Lost Villages

5 miles (8km) 1hr 45min **Ascent:** 130ft (40m)
Paths: Track and field, quiet lanes, ford or bridge, 2 stiles
Suggested map: OS Explorer OL45 The Cotswolds
Grid reference: SP 240362
Parking: Lay-bys on Todenham's main street, south of village hall

Walk among the ghosts of abandoned medieval agricultural communities.

❶ From lay-by below **Todenham village hall** walk up towards hall. Turn **L** just before it, along track that runs to R of house.

❷ After few paces go **R** up bank to gate. Go into field then straight across. Go through gate on far side, into field of undulations (medieval ploughing). Keep ahead to stile – cross into next field and, staying on its upper part, go ahead, in direction of house.

❸ Cross another stile and soon join farm track. Where track goes into field on R, keep ahead. At bottom of field path may become indistinct – look for small bridge, with gates at either end, amid undergrowth 50yds (46m) to **L**.

❹ Cross bridge then keep ahead, crossing field (site of **Ditchford Frary**) with farmhouse before you to R. On other side, go through gate, cross field and through gate to farm track.

❺ To see site of **Lower Ditchford**, turn **L** here and keep going over former railway line until you approach road – remains are to your L. Then return along track. Otherwise turn **R** on track and pass behind farmhouse. Track becomes metalled lane.

❻ Just before **High Furze Farm** turn **R** through gate into field. Follow its **L** margin until it dips down to **ford** across Knee Brook. Turn **R** here and after few paces find bridge on **L**.

❼ Cross then return to faint, grassy track that rises from ford. Stay on this line, with brook now to R, to reach gate in top corner. Go through to track that rises between 2 hedges. Parts of this may be boggy but soon track will become firmer and eventually take you to junction opposite entrance to **Todenham Manor**.

❽ Turn **R** here. Follow this track as it curves **L**, around manor, and finally brings you back to village with **village hall** on R. Turn **L** for **church** and **Farriers Arms** pub, **R** to return to car park.

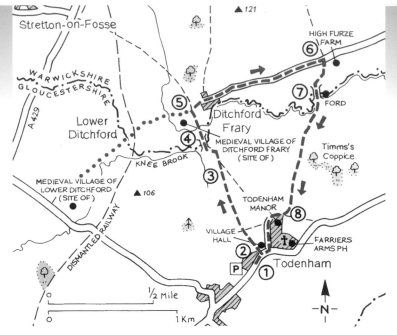

2 Sezincote A Taste of India

3 miles (4.8km) 1hr 15min **Ascent:** 85ft (25m)
Paths: Tracks, fields and lanes, 7 stiles
Suggested map: OS Explorer OL45 The Cotswolds
Grid reference: SP 175324
Parking: Street below Bourton-on-the-Hill church, parallel with main road

Discovering the influences of India through the Cotswold home of Sir Charles Cockerell.

❶ Walk up road from **telephone box** with **church** to your R. Turn **L** down signposted track between walls. Go through gate into field and then continue forward to pass through 2 more gates.

❷ Cross stile, followed by 2 kissing gates among trees. This is the **Sezincote Estate**. Its architecture and design was inspired, like many other buildings in the early 19th century, by the colourful aqua-tints brought to England from India by returning artists, such as William and Thomas Daniell. Built on the plan of a typical large country house, in every other respect it is thoroughly unconventional and owes a lot to Eastern influence, not least the large copper onion dome that crowns the house and the garden buildings. Go straight ahead, following markers and crossing drive. Dip down to gate among trees, with ponds on either side. Go ahead into field, from where **Sezincote House** is visible to R.

❸ Walk into next field and go right to end, aiming for top, **R-H** corner. Pass through gate to reach narrow road and turn **L**. Walk down this road, passing **keepers' cottages** to your L, and through series of gates. Road will bottom out, curve **L** and **R** and then bring you to **Upper Rye Farm**. Pass to R of farmhouse, go through gate and, immediately before barn, turn **L** along track and road.

❹ After 2nd cattle grid, go **L** over stile. Follow edge of field to footbridge. Go over it and turn **R**. Now follow **R-H** margin of field to stile in far corner. Cross this to follow path through woodland until you come to stile and field and continue on same line to another stile.

❺ Cross track to another stile and walk on. After few paces, with **Bourton-on-the-Hill** plainly visible before you, turn **R** and follow path to next corner. Turn **L** and pass through 3 gates. After 3rd one, walk on for few paces and turn **R** through gate to return to start.

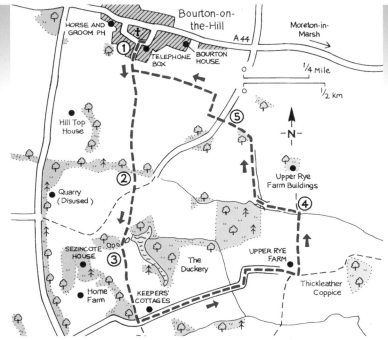

Bourton-on-the-Water A Wildlife Walk

4¾ miles (7.7km) 2hrs **Ascent:** 230ft (70m)

Paths: Track and field, can be muddy and wet in places, 26 stiles
Suggested map: OS Explorer OL45 The Cotswolds
Grid reference: SP 169208
Parking: Pay-and-display car park on Station Road

A walk on the wilder side.

❶ **Bourton-on-the-Water** can be very crowded during the summer with its river banks strewn with people picknicking and paddling – so arrive early or late to avoid the crowds. Opposite entrance to main pay-and-display car park in **Bourton-on-the-Water** locate public footpath and continue to junction opposite **cemetery**. Bear **R** to follow lane all the way to its end. There are 2 gates ahead. Take **R-H** gate, with stile beside it, on to grassy track.

❷ Follow track between lakes to where it curves **R**. Leave track to cross bridge and stile into field. Go across field, curving **R**, to come to stile at road.

❸ Cross road, turn **R** and immediately **L** on to track. After 100yds (91m) go **L** over stile into field. Turn **R**. Cross stile and return to track, with lake to **L**. Just before gate turn **R** over bridge and **L** over stile on to path alongside **River Windrush**. Continue until you reach stile at field. Turn **L**, cross another stile and go

L over bridge before turning **R** beside another lake.

❹ Where 2nd, smaller lake ends bear **R** to stile, followed by bridge and stile at field. Keep to **R** side of fields until you reach track. At house leave track and continue to stile. In next field, after 25yds (23m), turn **L** over stile then sharp **R**. Continue to stile then go half **L** across field. Continue on same line across next field to stile. Cross this; follow **R** margin of field, to climb slowly to junction of tracks. Turn **L** to visit **Clapton-on-the-Hill**, or turn **R** to continue.

❺ Follow track to field. Keep ahead then half **R** to pass **R** of woodland. Continue to stile, followed by 2 stiles together at field. Go half **L** to stile then follow succession of stiles, stream appearing to **L**.

❻ Cross bridge then go half **R** across field to bridge. Continue to more stiles then walk along grassy track towards houses. Cross one more stile and follow path to road in **Bourton**. Walk ahead to cross river. Turn **L**, then **R**, to return to start.

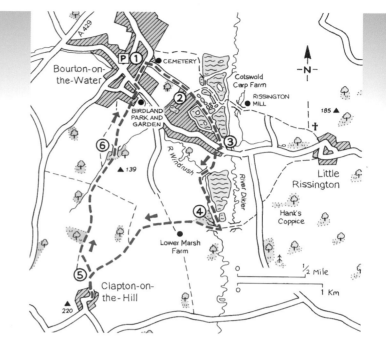

Blockley The Arboretum

4½ miles (7.2km) 2hrs **Ascent:** 410ft (125m)

Paths: Lanes, tracks and fields, 8 stiles
Suggested map: OS Explorer OL45 The Cotswolds
Grid reference: SP 165348
Parking: On B4479 below Blockley church

The exotic legacy of a 19th-century diplomat adorns this part of the Cotswold escarpment.

❶ Walk along road with church above you to your **R**. Continue ahead, pass **Brook House Cottage**, then turn **L** immediately, up lane. Follow this as it ascends for ¼ mile (400m) until it bears **L**.

❷ Continue ahead to pass **R-H** side of barn. Pass through gate and in next field follow its **R-H** boundary to another gate. Pass through this to stay on **L** side of next field. Pass into yet another field and then go half **R** to gate leading out to road.

❸ Turn **L** and follow road down to crossroads. Turn **R** to pass through **Batsford** village to junction (from where you can visit **church** on **R**). Bear **L**, and, at next junction, turn **R**.

❹ After few paces turn **R** on to footpath and follow this through succession of fields, negotiating stiles and gates where they arise. **Batsford House** will be visible above you to **R**.

❺ Finally, go through gate into ribbed field and turn **R** to stile just **L** of house at drive. This is the entrance to **Batsford Arboretum**, which offers 50 acres (20.3ha) of woodland containing over 1,000 species of trees and shrubs from all over the world, particularly from China, Japan and North America. Cross this entrance, pass through gate and follow path up field to stile. Cross and continue to track. Follow this up until where it bends **L**. Turn **R** on to path and almost immediately **L** at wall, to continue ascent. Keep going until you reach road.

❻ Cross road to go through gate and pass through 2 fields until you reach path among trees. Turn **L**, go through another gate, and, after a few paces, turn **R** over stile into field with **Blockley** below you. Continue down to stile at bottom. Cross into next field and pass beneath **Park Farm** on your **R**. Bear gently **L**, crossing stiles, along **Duck Paddle**, until you come to road. Turn **R** and return to your starting point in **Blockley**.

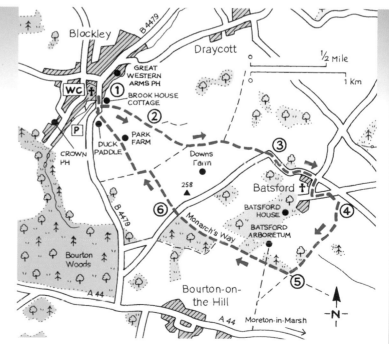

5 Chipping Campden Olimpick Playground

5 miles (8km) 2hrs **Ascent:** 280ft (85m)
Paths: Fields, roads and tracks, 8 stiles
Suggested map: OS Explorer OL45 The Cotswolds
Grid reference: SP 151391
Parking: Chipping Campden High Street or main square

From the Cotswolds' most beautiful wool town to Dover's Hill, the spectacular site of centuries-old Whitsuntide festivities.

❶ Turn **L** from Noel Arms, continue to Catholic **church**. Turn **R** into **West End Terrace**. Where this bears R, keep ahead on **Hoo Lane**. Follow this up to R turn, with farm buildings on L. Continue uphill over stile to path; keep going to a road.

❷ Turn **L** for few paces then **R** to cross to path. Follow this along field edge to stile. Go over to **Dover's Hill**. Follow hedge to stile with extensive views ahead. Turn **L** along escarpment edge, which drops away to your R. Pass **trig point** then **topograph**. Now go **R**, down slope, to kissing gate on **L**. Go through to road. Turn **R**.

❸ After 150yds (137m) turn **L** over stile into field. Cross and find gate in bottom **R-H** corner. Head straight down next field. At stile go into another field and, keeping to **L** of fence, continue to another stile.

Head down next field, cross track then find adjacent stiles in bottom **L** corner.

❹ Cross over 1st stile. Walk along bottom of field. Keep stream and fence to R and look for stile in far corner. Go over, crossing stream, then turn **L**, following rising woodland path alongside stream. Enter field through gate and continue to meet track. Stay on this, passing through gateposts, until you reach country lane. Turn **L**.

❺ After 400yds (366m) reach busier road. Turn **L** for 450yds (411m). Shortly before road curves L, drop down **R** on to field path parallel with road. About 200yds (183m) before next corner go half **R** down field to road.

❻ Turn **R**, down road. Shortly after cottage on R, go **L** into field. Turn **R** over stile and go half **L** to corner. Pass through kissing gate, cross road among houses and continue ahead to meet **West End Terrace**. Turn **R** to return to centre of **Chipping Campden**.

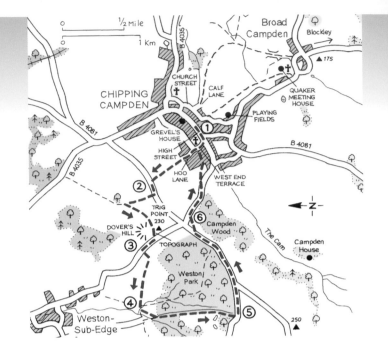

6 Guiting Power A Saxon Village

5 miles (8km) 2hrs **Ascent:** 295ft (90m)
Paths: Fields, tracks and country lanes, 10 stiles
Suggested map: OS Explorer OL45 The Cotswolds
Grid reference: SP 094245
Parking: Car park outside village hall (small fee)

A gentle ramble in from a typical village in quintessential Gloucestershire.

❶ From car park walk down road to village green. Cross road to walk down lane. At bottom go over stile into field. Turn **R**. Walk up bank, up to another stile. Don't cross one ahead but clamber over one to your **R** into field.

❷ Turn **L**. Walk straight across this field to another stile. Cross this and 2 more to pass farmhouse in **Barton** village. Follow lane down to larger road. Turn **R**. Cross bridge. Turn **L** up track and, after 100yds (91m), turn **R** up another track.

❸ After a few paces bear **L** and then walk along track for 1 mile (1.6km), until you reach another road. Turn **R**, walk along for 250yds (229m). Turn **L** on to track.

❹ Follow this all the way to road, past **quarry**. Cross road and then enter lane descending past house. This lane will bring you all the way into **Naunton**.

❺ At junction turn **R**. Walk through Naunton village and cross stone bridge by old mill, passing rectory to L and church concealed to R. (To get to **Black Horse Inn**, turn **L** and walk along street for 400yds (366m). Return by entering drive opposite pub, turning sharp R over stile, and walking back along side of river to emerge at road near church, where you turn **L**.) Continue up, out of village.

❻ After ¼ mile (400m) turn **R** over stile into field. Turn **L**, walk to stile and go into next field. Cross this field, enter next one. Follow path to **R** of trees to gate at road.

❼ Turn **R** along road. Continue to junction at bottom. Cross road to enter field and walk straight across. At end go down steps and pass to **R** of **pond**. Walk across next field then cross stile to walk to **L** of **church**. Before returning to the start take a look at the Norman doorway in **Guiting church**, it is an exceptionally rich golden hue.

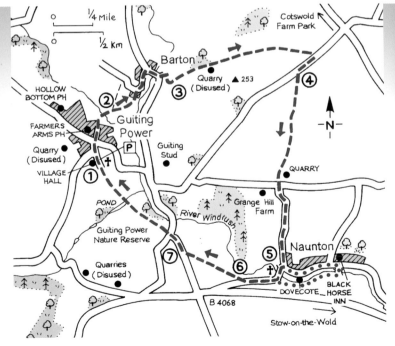

South Cerney The Cotswold Water Park

5 miles (8km) 2hrs Ascent: Negligible ⓘ

Paths:	Track, tow path and lanes, 10 stiles
Suggested map:	OS Explorer 169 Cirencester & Swindon
Grid reference:	SU 048974
Parking:	Silver Street, South Cerney

Ramble through an evolving landscape.

❶ From **Silver Street** walk north out of village. Immediately before turning to Driffield and Cricklade, turn **R** over stile on to bank. Stay on this for 800yds (732m), to reach brick bridge across path. Turn **R** up steps to reach narrow road.

❷ Turn **L**. Walk along for 200yds (183m) until you reach footpaths to R and L. Turn **R** along farm track, following signpost ('**Cerney Wick**'). Almost immediately remains of **Thames and Severn Canal** appear to L. When track veers R into farm, walk ahead over stile to follow path beneath trees – old canal tow path. At bridge keep ahead across stiles. Continue until you reach busy road.

❸ Cross with care. On far side you have 2 choices: continue on tow path or take path that skirts lakes. If you take lakeside path, you eventually rejoin tow path by going **L** at bridge after 600yds (549m). Continue until, after just under ½ mile (800m), you pass canal

roundhouse across canal to L and, soon after, reach lane at **Cerney Wick**.

❹ Turn **R**. Walk to junction at end of road, beside **Crown** pub. Cross to stile and enter field. Walk ahead to reach stile. Cross this aiming to **L** of cottage. Cross lane, go over another stile and enter field. Walk ahead and follow path as it leads across stile on to grass by lake. Walk around lake, going **R** then **L**. In corner before you, cross into field, walk ahead towards trees and cross stile to track.

❺ Turn **R**, rejoin old **railway line** and follow it all way to road. Cross this into car park. Go through gate on to track. Stay on this all the way to another road and follow path that runs to its **L**.

❻ Where path ends at beginning of **South Cerney**, continue along Station Road. Ignore footpath on R but turn **R** at 2nd one, which takes you across bridge and brings you to lane ('**Bow Wow**'). Turn **L** here between streams and return to **Silver Street**.

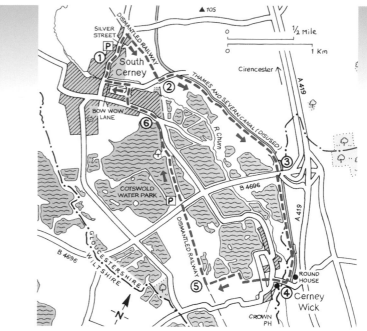

Hailes Abbey Thomas Cromwell and the Abbey

5 miles (8km) 2hrs Ascent: 605ft (185m) ⚠

Paths:	Fields, tracks, farmyard and lanes, 7 stiles
Suggested map:	OS Explorer OL45 The Cotswolds
Grid reference:	SP 050301
Parking:	Beside Hailes church

A walk exploring the countryside around Hailes Abbey, an important abbey destroyed by the King's Commissioner.

❶ From **Hailes church** turn **R**. Follow this lane to reach T-junction. Turn **R**. After 200yds (183m) turn **R** on to footpath. Cross area of concrete. Follow track as it goes **R** and **L**, becoming grassy path beside field. Go through gate, followed by stile. After 75yds (69m) turn **L**, through gate, and cross field to gate at road.

❷ Turn **R**. Follow road as it meanders through pretty village of **Didbrook** then stretch of countryside. At junction turn **R** for Wood Stanway. Walk through village into yard of **Glebe Farm**.

❸ At gate and stile cross into field. Walk ahead, looking for stile on L. You are now on **Cotswold Way**, well marked with arrows with white dot or acorn. Cross into field. Go half R, keeping to L of telegraph poles, to gap in hedge. Bear half **L** across next field, heading towards house. Cross stile. Turn sharp **R**, up slope, to

stile on your **R**. Cross this and turn immediately **L** up field. Go **L** over ladder stile by gate. Follow footpath as it wends its way gently up slope. At top keep ahead to gate at road.

❹ Turn **R** and **R** again through gate to track. Follow track, passing through gate, until at top (just before trees), you turn **R** to follow another track for 50yds (46m). Turn **L** through gate into field. Turn **R** to follow perimeter of field as it goes **L** and passes through gate beside Iron-Age fort, **Beckbury Camp**. Continue ahead to pass through gate (leading to **stone monument** with a niche).

❺ Turn **R** to follow steep path through trees. At bottom go straight across down field to gate. Pass through, continue down to another gate and, in field beyond, head down to stile beside signpost.

❻ Cross this and turn **R** down lane, all the way to road. To L is **Hayles Fruit Farm** (café). Continue ahead along road to return to **Hailes Abbey** and start.

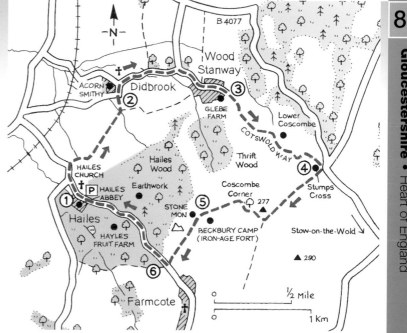

9 Winchcombe To Sudeley Castle

4 miles (6.4km) 2hrs **Ascent:** 490ft (150m) ▲2

Paths: Fields and lanes, 10 stiles

Suggested map: OS Explorer OL45 The Cotswolds

Grid reference: SP 024282

Parking: Free on Abbey Terrace; also car park on Back Lane

A walk above the burial place of Henry VIII's sixth queen – Catherine Parr.

❶ Walk towards village centre. Turn **R** on **Castle Street**. Where it levels out cross bridge. After few paces turn **L** on path between cottages. Pass into field and go half **R** to gate on other side.

❷ Turn **R** along lane. At end of stone wall, turn **L** into field. Go half **R** across field to find well-concealed gap in hedge, 50yds (46m) **L** of gateway, with plank across ditch. Cross then turn **L** to gate. Go through. Continue half **R** to another gap in hedge. Go through and keep ahead to protruding corner. Once you are round it, keep close to fence on L and continue into next corner to find (possibly overgrown) path leading to stile.

❸ Cross next field to another stile. Continue up following field to gate. Go through then go half **R** to far corner to stile (possibly concealed). Cross this then another stile almost immediately. Continue until you reach stile beside gate with stone barn above to R.

❹ Don't go over stile but turn **R** to head downhill to gate (at first hidden) in hedge 250yds (229m) below barn. Go through this on to track. Follow it as it curves towards house. Cross stile.

❺ Just before house turn **R**, cross field and go over stile. In next field go to bottom **L-H** corner to emerge on to road. Turn **L**. After few paces, turn **R** along lane, towards **Sudeley Lodge Parks Farm**.

❻ Opposite **cottage** turn **R** on to footpath across field. At bottom, cross stile. Turn **R**. At next corner turn **L**, remaining in same field. Cross another stile, continue for few paces then turn **R** over stile. Walk half **L**, following waymarkers to fence, with **Sudeley Castle** on R-H side.

❼ Go through 2 kissing gates to enter park area. Cross drive then field to another gate. Go through and bear half **R** to farthest corner. You will emerge on **Castle Street**, **Winchcombe**. Turn **L** to return to start in village centre.

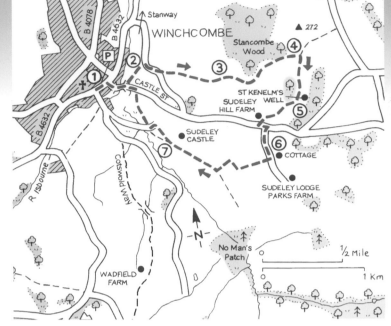

10 Slad Valley Walking with Rosie

4 miles (6.4km) 2hrs **Ascent:** 425ft (130m) ▲2

Paths: Tracks, fields and quiet lanes, 13 stiles

Suggested map: OS Explorer 179 Gloucester, Cheltenham & Stroud

Grid reference: SO 878087

Parking: Lay-by at Bull's Cross

Around Slad, backcloth to Laurie Lee's most popular novel, *Cider with Rosie*.

❶ From **Bull's Cross** walk to end of lay-by (going south). Turn **L** on to tarmac drive. Follow it down and, immediately before buildings, turn **L** over stile into field. Go half **R**, down field and up other side, to gate at top. Turn **L** along track. Where it joins another track stay **R** and continue to lane.

❷ Turn **R** and walk to bottom. Pass between **pond** and **Steanbridge Mill**. To visit Slad, follow lane into village. To continue, turn **L** immediately after **pond**. Continue to stile. Cross into field, with hedge on R. Continue to stile at top.

❸ Cross and follow path to another stile. Cross next field and another stile then continue as path curves **R** towards farm. Pass through gate on to track, stay to **R** of **Furners Farm** and curve **L**. About 30yds (27m) after curve turn **R** over stile on to wooded path then, after few paces, go **R** again over stile into field. Walk ahead, with farm above you to R. Cross another stile then keep to **R** of pond.

❹ At top of pond cross stile into field. Go half **L** across it to gate and stile. In next field, head straight across its lower part. At point where telegraph pole almost meets hedge, turn **R** over stile on to track. Turn **L** to reach lane.

❺ Turn **R**. Follow lane to valley bottom. Start to climb other side and at corner go over stile on **R**. Ascend steeply to another stile at road. Turn **R** along pavement. After 150yds (137m) cross to footpath and climb steeply. At junction of paths bear **L** and continue to field. Follow margin of field up then follow path as it weaves in and out of woodland.

❻ At top turn **R** on to **Folly Lane** and continue to junction. If you want to go into **Slad**, turn **R** otherwise continue on to path that will soon take you into woodland. Walk through woods, finally emerging at **Bull's Cross**.

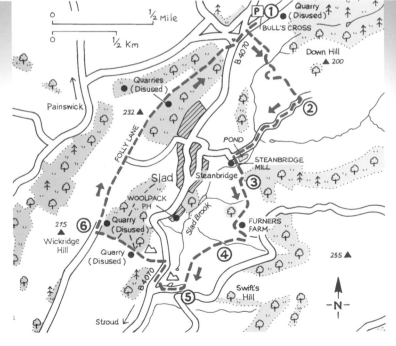

Chalford Weaving in the Stroud Valley

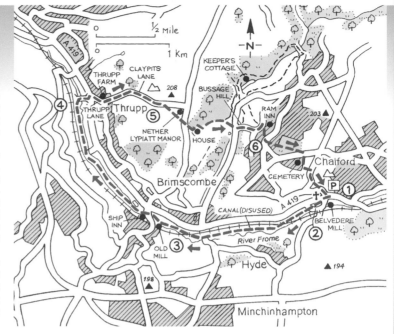

6 miles (9.7km) 3hrs **Ascent:** 495ft (150m)
Paths: Fields, lanes, canal path and tracks, 3 stiles
Suggested map: OS Explorer 168 Stroud, Tetbury and Malmesbury
Grid reference: SO 892025
Parking: Lay-by east of Chalford church

See the impact of the Industrial Revolution in the steep-sided Cotswold valleys.

❶ Walk towards **church**. Immediately before it, cross road and locate path going **R**, towards canal roundhouse. Note the **Belvedere Mill** on **L**. Follow tow path alongside **Thames and Severn Canal** (R).

❷ Cross road. Continue along tow path as it descends steps. Now follow path for about 2 miles (3.2km). It shortly disappears under railway line via culvert. Old mills and small factories line route.

❸ Shortly before reaching **Brimscombe**, path passes under railway again. Soon after, it becomes road into industrial estate. At road opposite mill turn **L**, to reach junction. Cross and turn **R**. Immediately after **Ship Inn** turn **L** along road among offices and workshops. Continue along path, with factory walls to R. Canal reappears (L). As you continue into country pass beneath 3 bridges and footbridge.

❹ At next bridge, with hamlet high on L, turn **R** to follow path to road. Cross this and turn **L**. After few paces turn **R** up short path to meet **Thrupp Lane**. Turn **R**. At top, turn **L** into **Claypits Lane**, turn **R** just before **Thrupp Farm** and climb steeply.

❺ After long climb, as road levels out, you will see **Nether Lypiatt Manor** ahead. Turn **R**, beside tree, over stile into field. Go half **L** to far corner. Cross stone stile. Follow narrow path beside trees to road. Descend lane steeply. Where it appears to fork, go ahead, to descend past a **house**. Enter woodland and fork **R** near bottom. Keep pond on L and cross road to climb **Bussage Hill**. After 100yds (91m) pass lane on L. At top fork **L**. Opposite **Ram Inn** turn **R**.

❻ After telephone box and bus shelter turn **L** to follow path among houses into woodland. Go ahead until you reach road. Turn **L** and immediately **R** down path beside **cemetery**. Descend to another road. Turn **R** for 50yds (46m); turn **L** down steep lane, leading back to **Chalford**. At bottom turn **L** to return to start.

Deerhurst Saxons and the Severn

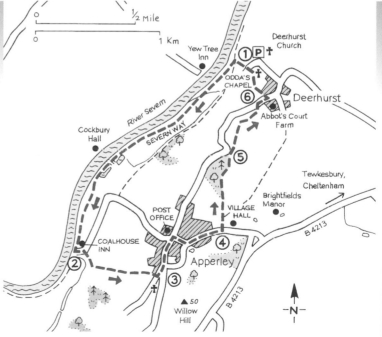

3¼ miles (5.3km) 1hr 30min **Ascent:** 115ft (35m)
Paths: Fields, pavement and river bank, 11 stiles
Suggested map: OS Explorer 179 Gloucester, Cheltenham & Stroud
Grid reference: SO 868298
Parking: Car park (small fee) outside Odda's Chapel

An easy walk to discover a rare Saxon chapel on the banks of the River Severn.

❶ With **Odda's Chapel** behind you, turn **L** then **R** through gate to walk along track as far as river bank. Here, turn **L** to follow **Severn Way**. Continue through number of gates and over stiles, following obvious path (sometimes overgrown), with river always close by on R. Eventually you reach **Coalhouse Inn**, set back a little to L.

❷ Turn **L** after pub to follow road. Once behind pub turn **R** through kissing gate on to area of rough grass. Go half **R** to stile and cross into field. Continue to another stile. In following field go uphill to find another stile at top, beside gate. Go over and follow **R-H** margin of field to another gate. Go through, and continue to road in **Apperley**.

❸ Turn **L** to walk through village. Opposite **post office** (which will be on your L) turn **R** down road with houses on your L.

❹ Just before **village hall** turn **L** and then walk across playing fields to stile. Cross it, and stay on same line to arrive at another stile. Now follow **R-H** margin of field as it eventually curves **R** and brings you to stile to lane.

❺ Go over stile on to lane and then turn sharp **R** to gate. Once in field turn **L** to come swiftly to another stile. Cross this to enter another field then walk down, crossing another stile and passing to **R** of house. Cross another stile (if there is one – it may only be a temporary measure) and then go half **L** to stile in hedge, well before **farm** ahead. Go over to road and then turn **R**.

❻ Continue until you come to concrete block on your **L**. Go up this and walk along ridge alongside private garden. Cross stile into meadow and continue diagonally **R** heading for stile and gate beside **Odda's Chapel** and timbered building next to it. This will bring you to gate by your starting point.

Ashleworth Medieval Tithes

7 miles (11.3km) 3hrs 15min **Ascent:** 65ft (20m)
Paths: Tracks, fields, lanes and riverbank, 16 stiles
Suggested map: OS Explorer 179 Gloucester, Cheltenham & Stroud
Grid reference: SO 818251
Parking: Grass verges in vicinity of tithe barn

Along the banks of the Severn, visiting a huge, and beautifully preserved, tithe barn.

❶ From **tithe barn** walk along road towards **River Severn**, passing **Boat Inn** on L-H side.

❷ Turn **L** over stile to walk along river bank. Follow it for just over 3 miles (4.8km). In general path is obvious, but where it sometimes appears to pass through gates, you may find gates are locked and that you should instead be using stile closer to river. **Sandhurst Hill** will come and go, followed by **Red Lion** pub (both across river).

❸ Eventually pass house. Immediately after it follow track that leads **L**, away from river then passes to **L** of houses and cottages. Track becomes lane and **Haw Bridge** will appear ahead.

❹ Just before lane goes L turn **L** over stile into field. Walk ahead then, as field opens up at corner, bear half **L** to reach stile. In next field, after few paces, turn **R** to cross bridge. Continue across 2 fields.

❺ This will bring you to lane. Cross it to walk down road opposite then, after 150yds (46m), look for bridge and stile concealed in hedge (**L**). Cross to field and aim half **R** to gateway in hedge. Continue on same line in next field and pass through gateway in corner to road.

❻ Turn **R** and pass **Great House**. Stay on lane as it bears **L**. After passing 2 houses, cross **L** into field. Head downhill, half **R**, to corner and rejoin lane.

❼ Turn **L**. Keep ahead into **Hasfield**, keeping **L** for **Ashleworth**. Turn **L** to see **church** then return to continue, via village, heading towards **Ashleworth**.

❽ Before cottages on R, turn **R** at footpath sign. Where path divides, take far **L** one across several fields on same line, passing L of **Colways Farm**. This will bring you to lane opposite turning for **Ashleworth Quay**. Just **L** of road opposite is stile into field. Cross it, then field to reach stile. Follow path on **R** side of fields all the way back to just before **tithe barn**.

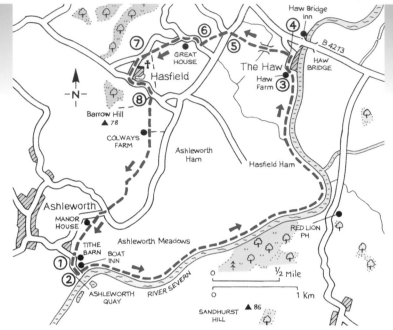

Uley Magnificent Fort on the Hill

3 miles (4.8km) 1hr 30min **Ascent:** 345ft (105m)
Paths: Tracks and fields
Suggested map: OS Explorer 168 Stroud, Tetbury and Malmesbury
Grid reference: ST 789984
Parking: Main street of Uley

The vast bulk of the ancient fort of Uley Bury forms the centrepiece for this walk along the Cotswold escarpment.

❶ From main street of Uley locate **post office** (on your **L** as you walk up street). Walk along narrow lane (to **R**, as you look at it). Pass between houses as lane dwindles to become track. Immediately before stile turn **R** along enclosed path towards **church**.

❷ When churchyard can be seen on R, turn **L** up narrow path beside cottage. This rises fairly sharply and brings you to kissing gate. Pass through into meadow. Climb steeply up grassland towards woodland.

❸ At tree-line keep **L** of woods. At corner go through gate and then follow winding woodland path, climbing among trees. When you come to fence stay on path as it bears **L**. Go over stile and then continue ascending, to emerge from woods. Stay on path as it rises across grassland to junction.

❹ Turn **R** to follow contour of hill – edge of ancient fort, **Uley Bury**. You are following perimeter of fort in anti-clockwise direction, with steep drops to your **R**. When you meet another junction of paths go **L** along edge of hill, with views to west.

❺ At next corner continue to follow edge of fort, disregarding stile that invites you to descend. At next corner, at fort's southeastern point, bear **R** on path that descends through hillocks and then quite steeply through bushes, keeping **L**. This will bring you to stile into meadow and tarmac path.

❻ Walk along path, all the way to cottage then kissing gate. Go through then pass beside cottage to arrive at lane. Turn **L** and follow it, soon passing **Uley Brewery**, which produces some fine beers including Uley Bitter and Uley Old Spot, to reach main road. Turn **L**, passing South Street, to return to start. If you want to sample the local beers, stop at the Old Crown pub on the main street opposite the **church**.

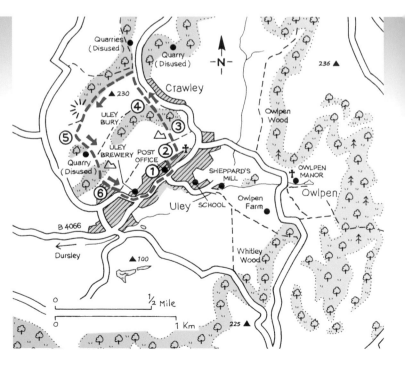

Adlestrop Empires and Poets

5 miles (8km) 2hrs Ascent: 230ft (70m)
Paths: Track, field and road, 6 stiles
Suggested map: OS Explorer OL45 The Cotswolds
Grid reference: SP 241272 **Parking:** Car park (donations requested) outside village hall

In the footsteps of imperialist Warren Hastings and the poet Edward Thomas.

1 From car park turn **L** along road. Pass road on R, bus shelter (**Adlestrop**) and houses. 200yds (183m) after another road, turn **R** over stile. Follow woodland path to **L**. Continue on path until it meets stile at road.

2 Cross road with care. Turn **L** along verge. Before road on R, turn **R** through gate to path in **Daylesford Estate**. Path curves **L** towards fence. Stay to **L** of fence until you reach stile. Go over and cross paddock. Pass through gate, turn **R** then **L** between fences.

3 Cross bridge. Follow avenue towards buildings. Traverse farmyard; turn **R**, passing estate office.

4 Walk along drive between paddocks, soon following estate wall. Pass gateway to offices then, as it goes sharp **R**, stay on drive, eventually reaching road. Turn **R**.

5 Walk along road, with estate R, until **Daylesford** estate village. Opposite **Daylesford House** drive is footpath leading to **Daylesford church**. After visiting church, return to road, turn **R** and retrace your steps. Before pavement ends, turn **R** over stile.

6 Cross field to railway footbridge. Go over it and ahead into field (not field on L) then head, bearing slightly **R**, for another footbridge. Cross into field, turn **R** then **L** at corner. Follow field margin as it passes into another field. At next corner, enter field in front of you. Turn **R** then **L**. At next corner, go **R** to track.

7 Turn **R** and pass **Oddington church**. Continue to junction. Turn **R**. Pass **Fox** pub and continue to next junction. Turn **R** and walk along pavement. Where this ends, cross road carefully on pavement opposite.

8 Beyond bridge, turn **L** along Adlestrop road then turn immediately **R** over 2 stiles. Walk towards **Adlestrop Park**. As you draw level with **cricket pitch** go diagonally **L** to gate about 100yds (91m) to R of pavilion.

9 Follow track past **Adlestrop church**. At next junction turn **L** through village until you reach bus stop. Turn **L** to car park.

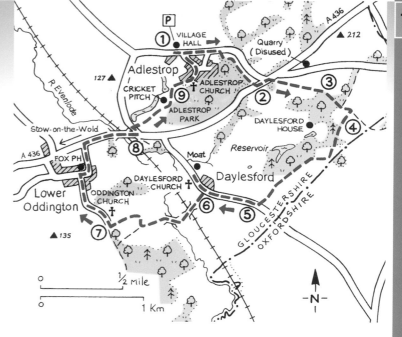

Ashperton Hereford's Lost Canal

7¾ miles (12.5km) 3hrs 30min Ascent: 260ft (79m)
Paths: Field and woodland paths, minor roads, at least 35 stiles
Suggested map: OS Explorer 202 Leominster & Bromyard
Grid reference: SO 642415
Parking: St Bartholomew's Church, Ashperton

Along an old waterway, now being restored.

1 From car park take 'forty shillings' gate, behind houses. (For 10 paces path is in a garden.) Join track to A417. Turn **L**, then **R**, beside driveway. Follow fingerpost across meadows for 600yds (549m). Find gate by cricket net. Veer **R**. Cross driveway down field. Join Haywood Lane near house. Turn **L**. Follow this for 1 mile (1.6km). Find stile on **L** just beyond gate, 100yds (91m) after driveway to **Upleadon Court**.

2 Cross arable fields and ditch, then **Upleadon Farm's** driveway. Aim for far **L-H** corner. Skirt woodland to L, later striking **L** (waymarked) up huge field. At **Gold Hill Farm** go **R** of tall shed. Behind this, turn **L** then briefly up and **R**. Follow boundary to road.

3 Turn **L** for ¼ mile (400m). Where road turns **L** continue for ½ mile (800m), initially beside wood. Over rotting plank turn **L** but in 25yds (23m) turn **R**. After 500yds (457m) enter trees. On leaving them strike half **R** for **White House**.

4 Turn **R** along road. At junction, take footpath opposite (ditch on R). (Beware of hitting your head on horizontal tree trunk just after single-plank footbridge.) Walk 700yds (640m) across fields, over 3 footbridges and under power lines, passing through gap to stile, but do not cross – note 3 waymarkers on its far side. Turn **L**, heading towards old orchards. Just beyond **Homend** find stile in far **L-H** corner, shielded by ash and elder. Turn **L**, soon moving **R** to double gates flanking wide concrete bridge. After avenue keep ahead, eventually veering **R**. Go 550yds (503m), crossing driveway to **Canon Frome Court**, then another track, finally reaching road by spinney.

5 Cross road; walk to canal. Turn **L**. In 140yds (128m) turn **R**, over canal. Veer **L** and uphill, finding large oak in top **L-H** corner. Keep this line despite field boundary shortly curving away. At copse turn **R**, later moving **L** into indistinct lane. Village hall heralds A417. Turn **L**, along pavement then **R** to church.

17 Frome Valley Two Churches

4¾ miles (7.7km) 2hrs 30min **Ascent:** 475ft (145m) ⚠

Paths: Field paths, dirt tracks, lanes and minor roads, 14 stiles

Suggested map: OS Explorer 202 Leominster & Bromyard

Grid reference: SO 679502

Parking: Roadside just before grassy lane to Acton Beauchamp's church – please tuck in tightly

You'll discover secluded churches and special wild service trees set amid pastures on this easy ramble.

❶ Leave churchyard by iron gate in top corner. Soon enter orchard. Skirt round to **R**, passing outbuildings of **Church House Farm** and then down to pass behind tall barns. Now orchard track ascends. When 110yds (100m) beyond power lines, at corner of plantation, turn **L** (blue waymarker), to walk between orchard rows. At end turn **L**. In roughly 160yds (146m), well before power lines and just before trees shielding pond, go **R**. Soon you'll have hedge on your **L**; reach gate and stile of 3 railway sleepers.

❷ Once through **Halletshill Coppice** drop straight down to footbridge. Now go straight up bank, swapping hedge sides, to minor road. Turn **R**. Take the opportunity to visit the **church**. You will notice that the stonework is of a similar vintage to that in **Acton Beauchamp** – Norman and 13th century. Return to

road and turn **R**. At entrance to **The Hawkins** take stile, then follow waymarkers across track to skirt this farm. Now head down pastures to cross footbridge over **Linton Brook**.

❸ Turn **L**, walking beside **Linton Brook** for ⅝ mile (1km), to road. Turn **L** for 160yds (146m). Turn **R**. Now driveway to **Upper Venn Farm** runs for ½ mile (800m). Just before farm buildings move **L**, to stile roughly 70yds (64m) along edge of field from farm.

❹ Cross field diagonally, to gate in **L** hedge. Turn **L** across field, aiming slightly uphill, beside residual mature oaks. You'll find stile beyond electricity pole. Pick up rough track to **The Venn**. Admire its cream walls and exposed timbers and then turn away, along drive. Follow this down to minor road.

❺ Turn **L**, passing **Frome Valley Vineyard** on a sharp bend. At crossroads go straight over. Climbing this quite steep lane, **Church of St Giles** comes into view. Take 1st turning on **L** to return to your car.

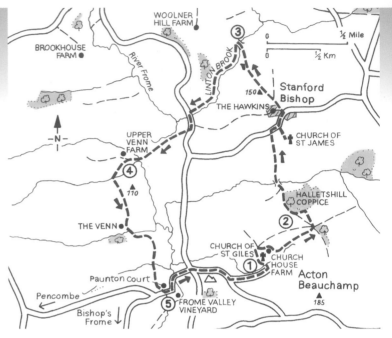

18 Coppet Hill Beside the River Wye

6¾ miles (10.9km) 3hrs **Ascent:** 855t (260m) ⚠

Paths: Quiet lanes, riverside meadows, woodland paths, 2 stiles

Suggested map: OS Explorer OL14 Wye Valley & Forest of Dean

Grid reference: SO 575196

Parking: Goodrich Castle car park open daily 9:30am to 7pm

A peaceful walk with fine views.

❶ Walk back to castle access road junction; turn **L**. In 125yds (114m) cross bridge over **B4229**.

❷ Go up further 400yds (366m). Ignore another road branching off to **R**, and go on just a few paces – there are 3 low wooden posts to your **L**.

❸ Opposite, between 2 roads, sign ('**Coppet Hill Nature Reserve**') indicates return route. Go ½ mile (800m) up this dead end, to cattle grid. Here, at brow, woods give way to parkland. Go ahead for 275yds (251m) to single horse chestnut tree at **R** turn.

❹ Continue for 400yds (366m), bending **L** and dipping down, along road. It curves **R** slightly, while gravel track goes up ramp and slightly **L**.

❺ Curve **R**. Ignore pillared driveway but go down **youth hostel's** driveway. At its entrance gate take footpath that runs initially parallel to it. Go down wooden steps and along sometimes muddy path to reach T-junction beside **River Wye**.

❻ Turn **R**, following Wye Valley Walk (turn **L** to visit **church** first). Within ¼ mile (400m) you'll reach old, iron girder railway bridge, which now carries Wye Valley Walk across river, but stay this side, passing underneath bridge. After walking 125yds (114m) look out for 6 wooden steps down to **L** at fork.

❼ Take steps, to remain close to river. Continue for about 1¼ miles (2km). Enter **Coldwell Wood** to walk beside river for further ¼ mile (400m). On leaving, keep by river in preference to path that follows woodland's edge. In about 350yds (320m) you'll reach stile beside fallen willow.

❽ Turn **R** ('**Coppet Hill**'). Soon begin arduous woodland ascent. Eventually you'll have some fine views. Path levels, later rising to **The Folly**, then goes down (not up!) to triangulation point. Follow clear green sward ahead, becoming narrow rut then stepped path, down to road, close to Point ❸. Retrace your steps to castle car park.

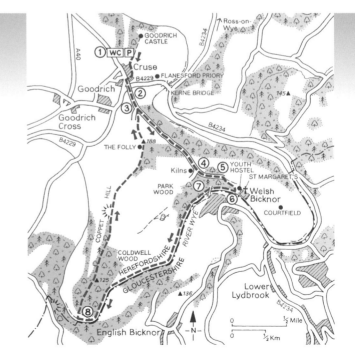

Aymestrey Rocks of Ages

4¾ miles (7.7km) 2hrs 30min Ascent: 525ft (160m)

Paths: Good tracks, field paths, minor roads, steep woodland sections, 11 stiles
Suggested map: OS Explorer 203 Ludlow
Grid reference: SO426658
Parking: At old quarry entrance, on east side of A4110, ¼ mile (400m) north of Aymestrey Bridge

Around a redeveloped quarry now used for grazing and woodland.

❶ Walk up access road for almost ½ mile (800m), until beyond garden of house and just before junction of tracks. Note stile on **R** – your route returns over this.

❷ Go 30yds (27m) further and turn **L**, passing house with stone wall relic in its garden. Continue, through **Yatton**, to T-junction. Turn **L** to **A4110**. Cross to stile, walking along **L-H** field edge. Through gate go forward then skirt round **R** edge of oak and ash embankment, to find corner stile. Walk up **L** edge of field but, at brow, where it bends for 70yds (64m) to corner, slip **L** through gap in hedge to walk along its other side. Within 60yds (55m) you will be on clear path, steeply down through woodland, ravine on your **L**. Join driveway of **River Bow**, to minor road.

❸ Turn **L** here, joining **Mortimer Trail**. Continue along riverside lane for nearly ¾ mile (1.2km), to reach A4110. Cross then walk for 25yds (23m) to **R**.

(**Riverside Inn** is 175yds/160m further.) Take raised green track, heading for hills. Then go diagonally across 2 fields, to stile and wooden steps.

❹ Ascend steeply through trees. Leave by stile, to cross 2 meadows diagonally. Take stile on **R** to walk along **L-H** edge of field, still heading downhill. At trees turn **L**. Soon reach tarmac road. Turn **L** along road, now going back uphill. Beyond **Hill Farm**, enter Croft Estate. Walk along gravel track. After 110yds (100m) ignore R fork but, 550yds (503m) further on, you must leave it. This spot is identified by end to deciduous trees on L and **Mortimer Trail** marker post on wide ride between larches and evergreens on R.

❺ Turn **L** (no signpost). Within 110yds (100m) go half **R** and more steeply down. Within 250yds (229m) look out for modern wooden gate, waymarked, leading out of woods. Walk along its **R-H** edge (and beside small plantation). At far corner, within field, turn **L** to Point ❷. Retrace your steps to start.

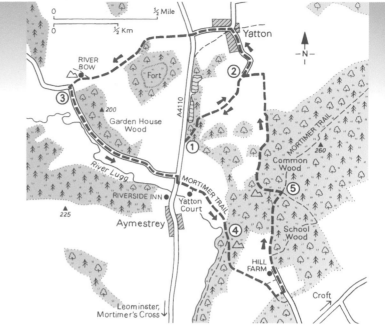

Kilpeck Orcop Hill

4¾ miles (7.7km) 2hrs 45min Ascent: 590ft (180m)

Paths: Field paths, tracks and minor lanes, 21 stiles
Suggested map: OS Explorer 189 Hereford & Ross-on-Wye
Grid reference: SO 445304
Parking: Spaces beside St Mary's and St David's Church, Kilpeck

A walk once enjoyed by Violette Szabo, a wartime heroine.

❶ Walk down to **Red Lion**. Turn **R**. At junction follow 'Garway Hill'. Take 2nd fingerpost. Find another stile behind **The Knoll** (house). Strike diagonally across pasture. Cross another stile, now with field boundary on your **R**. Veer **L** to reach lane at bend. Turn **L**. Follow waymarkers through trees then go straight down field to near junction.

❷ Turn **L**, past **Two Brooks**. After 500yds (457m) turn **L**, through gate by **Grafton Oak**, tucked behind. Soon in meadow, follow fence until crossing stile. Now keep ahead but drift down, guided by gigantic oak. The stile you need is ahead, not another, further down, that crosses brook. Contour with trees on your **L** for 2 fields. In 3rd find footbridge down and **L**.

❸ Follow waymarkers, diagonally up field. Walk with wire fence on your **R**. Leave this long field at its top end (but, to observe rights of way, first cross and re-

cross wire fence on your **R**, via wooded area). Go diagonally to opening beside hollow oak, not more easily seen, 3-bar stile. Move **L** to walk along **L-H** field edge. Ignore waymarker into **L-H** field – any way out has completely disappeared. Instead keep ahead, to tarmac road. Turn **L**. After 650yds (594m) fingerpost slants **L**.

❹ Take this path through bracken to track. Turn **R** for 25yds (23m), then **L**, to pass to **R** of **Saddlebow Farm**. Avenue below leads into field. Walk along this **R** edge, to just before gate. Join good track, following it for 650yds (594m), until 3 gates in corner.

❺ Take 2nd on **L**. Beyond **New House Farm** go over ¼ mile (400m) to junction. Don't turn down to Kilpeck yet! Go 160yds (146m) further. Here go **L**, around old farm buildings. Descend to unseen gap not 50yds (46m) **L** of bottom **R-H** corner. Out of this copse, cross 2 fields to pass between buildings of **The Priory**. Avenue of horse chestnuts leads to **Red Lion**.

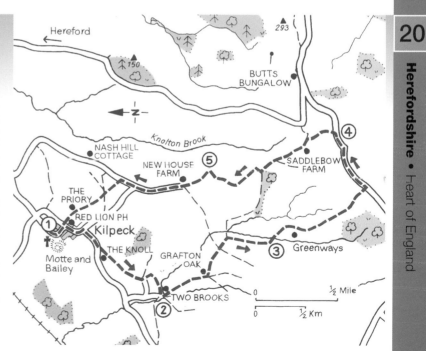

21 Abbey Dore Golden Valley

8 miles (12.9km) 3hrs 45min **Ascent:** 540ft (165m) 🛆
Paths: Meadows, tracks and woodland paths (one stony, awkward descent), 24 stiles
Suggested map: OS Explorer OL13 Brecon Beacons (East)
Grid reference: SO 386302 **Parking:** On east side of B4347, south of lychgate, facing south

In search of a 19th-century workhouse.

❶ Cross B4347 at lychgate. Slant **L** up fields. Beside dwelling go up path, to 3rd field, then corner stile. In 20yds (18m) turn **R** up hedged lane to **Ewyas Harold Common**.

❷ This is the prescribed route but dozens of paths and tracks criss-cross here. Across concrete track take **L** diagonal ride. In 65yds (60m) take slightly **L** option. After 45yds (41m) bear **R**. In 325yds (297m) take **R-H** option. After 70yds (64m) move **L** slightly to resume your line. In 160yds (146m) move 10yds (9m) **L** on wide track; turn **R**. In 55yds (50m) turn **L** on big gravel track. Just beyond seat fork **R**, down rutted track. After 3 houses swing **R**, over cattle grid.

❸ In village, turn **R** then **R** again. At bend go up steps. Aim **L** of spinney. After buildings ascend 3 fields to corner stile. When trees end swing up and **L** to boundary corner. Keep field edge R, to **Plash Farm**.

❹ Get behind farmhouse by turning **R** twice. Descend to bottom corner. Sunken lane leads to road.

Turn **R**, then **L** to **Dulas Court**. Cross brook by bridge beside buildings. Turn **R** in 30yds (27m). Go diagonally up meadow into conifers. Walk uphill for 50yds (46m) to track, but, within 30yds (27m), clear path bears **R**, uphill. Out of woodland, aim for pole. Pass between buildings of **Cot Farm**.

❺ Walk with hedge L. Keep this line across fields, to regain common. In 70yds (64m) join track (L part of hairpin); 70yds (64m) further continue on green sward, soon joining another track. Some 50yds (46m) before common, which you saw earlier, turn **L**. Stiles over deer fences lead to lane by **Cwm Farm**. Turn **R**. Before **Abbey Dore Court Garden** find stile at bridge. In 3rd field after 300yds (274m) move **R** to cross bridge.

❻ Waymarked stiles lead to **Riverdale** (Dore workhouse buildings). Retrace your steps to Point ❻. Now keep on east side of river. Turn **L** at road. In 60yds (55m) take well-waymarked route between military fence and gardens. Finally, concrete footbridge, meadow and agricultural graveyard lead to **abbey**.

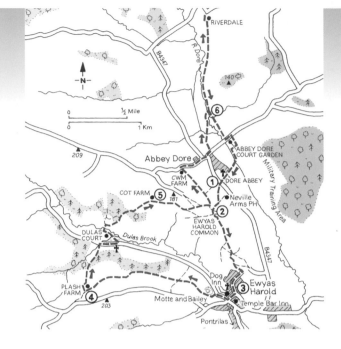

22 Clifford Original Settlement

5½ miles (8.8km) 2hrs 30min **Ascent:** 560ft (171m) 🛆
Paths: Field paths and lanes, awkward embankment, over 30 stiles
Suggested map: OS Explorer 201 Knighton & Presteigne
Grid reference: SO 251450 **Parking:** Roadside parking at St Mary's Church, Llanfair

A 'backwater' of the River Wye.

❶ Just after road junction at corner of churchyard, take steps on **R**. Yellow arrows indicate route. Leave **Ton Wood** by gate on **L**, beside wire game-breeding enclosure. More arrows lead across old railway towards **Clifford**. Leave last meadow beside house.

❷ Walk to road. Turn **L** then **R** for **castle**. Retrace your steps to Point ❷. Take arrow pointing to oaks. At tarmac beyond follow 'Unsuitable for heavy goods vehicles'. On **R**, after 440yds (402m) find stile (hidden) and go up steep metal gate steps – easier is metal gate 30yds (27m) before stile. Across this green strip scramble down and up railway embankment. Halfway up field switch hedge from your **L** to **R**. Find stile behind derelict harvester. Wooded path soon reaches lane.

❸ Turn **L**. In 230yds (210m), before sheds, strike **R**, to stile behind 6 hawthorns in dip. Through garden, take rough track joining 2 tarmac lanes. Turn **R** for 30 paces. Waymarker points towards stile in trees. Go down this field to meet lane.

❹ Turn **L**; continue for ½ mile (800m) to B4352. Turn **R**. In 70yds (64m) cross to stile into meadow. Aim to **R** of trees on skyline then stile by house.

❺ Walk through garden. Take bridleway, **R**. After leafy interlude join stony track, but within 160yds (146m), where footpath crosses, turn **R**, to reach **Holy Trinity Church**.

❻ Retrace your steps to Point ❺. Go diagonally **L** to stile hidden by hedge. Turn **R**, around 2 sides of field. In next turn **R**, along field edge. Take driveway near by. At **Hardwicke Court** step around wall to walk **R** beside building, down path on lawn. At bottom, through small gate, maintain line, although 'Road Used as a Public Path' is obliterated. At farm gate keep ahead, past gigantic oak, to find wicket gate – 'RUPP' becomes more defined. Don't take waymarked stile 40yds (37m) to **R**. At **Hardwicke Mill** go into garden. Leave by stile on **R**. Ascend field edge, striking **L** at trees. Having skirted to **R** of house, you'll see **St Mary's Church** across fields ahead. Head for church.

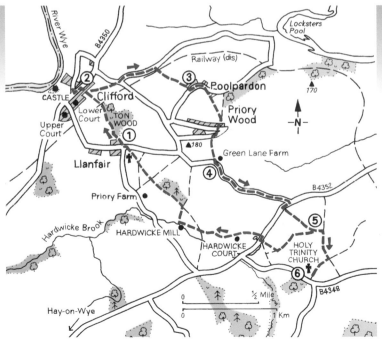

Golden Valley Honey Country

6 miles (9.7km) **3hrs Ascent:** 1,165ft (355m)

Paths: Minor lanes, good tracks, meadows, couple of short but severe descents over grass, 24 stiles

Suggested map: OS Explorer 201 Knighton & Presteigne or OL13 Brecon Beacons (East)

Grid reference: SO 313416 (on Explorer 201) **Parking:** Car park beside Dorstone Post Office

Across a heavenly landscape.

1 Go down near side village green but turn **R** (not to church), passing houses. At lane end turn **L**, passing D'Or Produce Ltd. At **B4348** care is required. Continue, bridging **River Dore**. Be sure to switch sides before road bends severely **R**. Follow driveway towards **Fayre Way Stud Farm**. Clearly waymarked route across pastures leads up to **Arthur's Stone**.

2 Beyond **Arthur's Stone** take route signed by fingerpost. Cross 2nd field diagonally. Follow **L** side of fence to stile **L** of the corner. After 2 fields descend very steeply on grass beside larches. Keep beside hedge to find awkward stile. Take lane but skirt **R** of **Finestreet Farm** using several stiles. In another steep meadow find stile below and **L** of massive oak with fallen one beside it. Cross field diagonally, to pass beside timber-framed house. Beyond is **Bredwardine**.

3 Cross road carefully. In 80yds (73m) avenue leads to **St Andrew's Church**. At very end, stile and waymarkers lead to Bredwardine's bridge.

4 Go back to Point **3**. Take '25%' gradient road beside **Red Lion Hotel**. Go 700yds (640m) up lane, including steepest section, to just before **Hill Cottage**. Fingerpost points R, and behind you is '1 in 4' sign.

5 Keep ahead, ignoring R turn after 160yds (146m). When road rises sharply after stream, find gate **R**, just past house ('Finestreet Dingle'). Now ascend dell (also called Finestreet Dingle) guided by blue arrows. In front of house turn **L** then **L** again, to skirt plantation. Row of hawthorns points to stile near brow. Tackle awkward gate near scrawny pines, keeping this line to minor road. Turn **R**. In 325yds (297m) turn **L** ('20%'). After another 325yds (297m) find fingerpost, hidden behind holly tree.

6 Soon join track visible ahead. Continue to and through **Llan Farm**. However, 220yds (201m) beyond it, take diagonal footpath (not old lane, R). Cross sunken lane, old **railway**, then village playing fields to reach road near church. Cross then skirt **R** of churchyard, along fenced path, to village green.

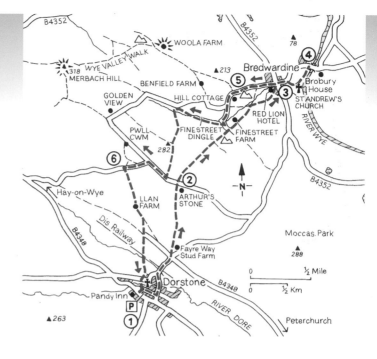

Cleeve Hill A Fruity Route

4½ miles (7.2km) **2hrs Ascent:** 225ft (69m)

Paths: Paths across fields, stony tracks and village roads, 8 stiles

Suggested map: OS Explorer 205 Stratford-upon-Avon & Evesham

Grid reference: SP 077469

Parking: Outside Littleton Village Hall, School Lane, Middle Littleton (tithe barn parking for visitors only)

Walking in Victoria plum country.

1 Walk westwards up School Lane to B4085, here called Cleeve Road. Cross diagonally **L** to take rutted, stony track, screened by hedgerow from **Kanes Foods**. At junction of tracks turn **R** to pass beside gate, following blue arrow. After 328yds (300m) reach opening **R** and line of plum trees making field boundary; on **L** is stile.

2 Cross it, entering Worcestershire Wildlife Trust's **Windmill Hill Nature Reserve**. Descend, ignoring crossing tracks, to another stile and across 1 field to B4510. Follow footpath ('Cleeve Prior') through **caravan site**. (Keep on road for 220yds/201m for **Fish and Anchor**.) Take stile out of caravan park to walk on stone track beside river.

3 At fenced log cabin with lanterns and basketball net, move to **R** to take double-stiled footbridge – don't be deterred by sign 'OPAC Private Fishing' – and resume riverside stroll. Continue through mostly ungated pastures. Go through small iron gate, leave river by taking **R-H** fork. Ascend through trees to clearing and path junction.

4 Turn **R**, back on yourself, soon walking into trees again, to follow bridleway. In just under 1 mile (1.6km) B4510 cuts through hill, beside **The Hills**. Cross to fingerpost, but follow path for just 75yds (69m).

5 Climb stile into nature reserve here, and follow waymarked, contouring path. After 440yds (402m) you'll recognise your outward route. Turn **L** here, up bank, retracing your steps for just 30yds (27m), to Point **2**. Once at top go straight across, walking with line of plum trees on your **L**. When this ends, maintain this direction to B4085, **tithe barn** making clear objective ahead.

6 Cross road and go straight ahead. Before young trees take stile or gate to **R**. In 15yds (14m) turn **L** to visit tithe barn, or turn **R** to reach village road. Turn **R** again, shortly to start.

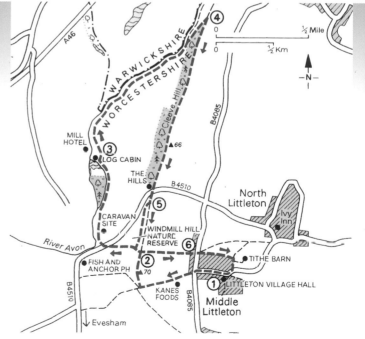

25 Tardebigge The Ups and Downs

5½ miles (8.8km) 2hrs 30min **Ascent:** 295ft (90m) ⚠
Paths: Tow path, pastures, field paths and minor lanes, 21 stiles
Suggested map: OS Explorer 204 Worcester & Droitwich Spa
Grid reference: SO 974682
Parking: Limited space, so park tightly and considerately, on north and east side of road bridge

Visit Worcestershire's famous big wet steps.

❶ Cross bridge No 51 and turn **L**, taking tow path on south side. Follow this until about 15yds (14m) before next bridge – No 52.

❷ Turn **R** here, into trees, then down field. Cross double-stiled footbridge among trees then keep ahead, over driveway to **Patchetts Farm**. Skirt copse to L, then another stile and 2-plank bridge. Cross 2 fields, keeping hedge on your L. You will reach gate on your **L**, close to broken oak tree with substantial girth.

❸ Turn **R**. Within 110yds (100m) go through gate ahead (no waymarker), ignoring gate to L. Go a quarter **R** (or skirt crops) to find stile. Retain this diagonal line to cross footbridge of 3 planks, then find rickety, narrow stile in next field's corner. Walk with hedge on your L to reach minor road junction. Turn **R** for 55yds (50m). Turn **L** to walk across 3 more fields to dilapidated metal gate. Now take **R-H** field edge to reach minor road.

❹ Turn **R**. Follow this for ½ mile (800m) to **Lower Bentley Farm's** driveway. Go 140yds (128m) further, to fingerpost on **R**. Cross pastures by gaps in hedgerows, later with hedge on your L, but veer to stile in **R-H** corner at end. Cross this, then double stile, go three-quarters **L** to road.

❺ Turn **R**, and in 75yds (69m) turn **L**. Here, beyond awkward ditch, is new kissing gate with latch. Cross pastures easily towards **Orchard Farm**, but then turn **R**, away from it. Over corner stile go straight ahead. At double stile (across ditch) go half **L**, and at gap in hedge turn **R**. Now turn **L** without gaining height for 650yds (594m), aiming to **L** of black-and-white house, for stile and gate. In 80yds (73m) reach road.

❻ Turn **R**. At T-junction turn **L**. Join canal tow path this side of Stoke Pound Bridge. (The **Queen's Head** is on other side.) Now you have over ¾ mile (1.2km) to return to your car at road bridge, approximately mid-way up **Tardebigge Flight**.

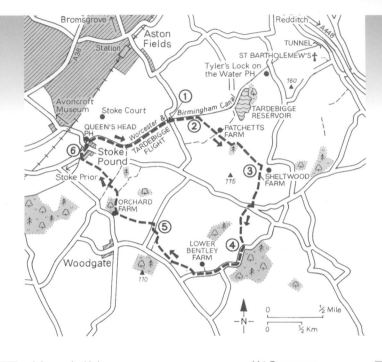

26 Hanbury Hall The Ice Houses

4¾ miles (7.7km) 2hrs 15min **Ascent:** 250ft (76m) ⚠
Paths: Meadows, tracks and easy woodland paths, 17 stiles
Suggested map: OS Explorer 204 Worcester & Droitwich Spa
Grid reference: SO 957652
Parking: Piper's Hill car park, on B4091 between Stoke Works and Hanbury (fast road and no sign)

A stroll around an estate park.

❶ From bottom of car park, follow driveway to **Knotts Farm**. Go ahead on **L-H** (1 of 2 parallel paths). 350yds (320m) after farm reach track at fingerpost.

❷ Keep ahead, with field boundary on L. Ascending towards **church**, reach stake with 2 waymarkers.

❸ Fork **L**, soon passing spinney, then losing height across meadow. Take care as stile and steps here spill you straight on to minor but fast road. Cross then go beside **school**. Ahead, when 20yds (18m) before stile out of 3rd field, turn **R**, aiming just to L of young, fenced oak. Cross wobbly stile. In 70yds (64m) cross footbridge on **L**. Cross 2 stiles to Pumphouse Lane.

❹ Turn **R**. Take stile and gate close to black-and-white **Grumbleground Cottage**. In 40yds (37m) cross 3-plank footbridge. Ascend slightly, in line with electricity poles. After 2 fields turn **R**, alongside wire fence. Reach road.

❺ Cross road to footpath opposite. At stile go half **L**,

guided by solitary, fenced conifer. Pass close to **Hanbury Hall's** entrance, easing away from perimeter wall to cross large field to corner.

❻ Ignore minor road, turning immediately **R**. Hug boundary fence of coppice. Continue down **R-H** field edge. At junction turn **R** at National Trust sign, into this former deer park. After just 50yds (46m), at small drainage ditch, edge **R**, along slight green hollow. After another 110yds (100m), where it curves R, leave hollow to keep line. Aim for stile about 300yds (274m) away, to **L** of clump of fenced trees, which hides round pond. Maintain this line going up incline – **Hanbury church** is seen on L – to reach tarmac driveway.

❼ Turn **L**. When it curves R go straight ahead to walk in oak avenue. Keep this line for 700yds (640m), to minor road. Turn **R**, then **L** up to church. In churchyard walk round perimeter, down to kissing gate. Shortly rejoin outward route at Point **❸**. Remember to go **L**, into woods, at Point **❷**.

Clent Hills A Treat in Springtime

3½ miles (5.7km) 2hrs **Ascent:** 660ft (200m) ⚠
Paths: Woodland paths (sometimes muddy), tracks, 8 stiles
Suggested map: OS Explorer 219 Wolverhampton & Dudley
Grid reference: SO 938808
Parking: National Trust pay-and-display car park, Nimmings Wood

A brief circuit of the most visited hills in Worcestershire and where, in spring, fields of oilseed rape flood the landscape with colour.

❶ Return to car park entrance and turn **R** for few paces. Cross road to stile and take **L-H** of 2 options. Immediately you'll see striking urban panorama. Descend steadily but, at cylindrical wooden post, turn **R** (with waymarker). Continue across fields, probably populated with horses, until kissing gate. Here take forward option (not **R** fork), to reach churchyard of **St Kenelm's** in Romsley parish. It may appear to be 'overgrown' since it is managed like a traditional hay meadow.

❷ Leave by lychgate. Turn **L** along road for short distance, then **R** at T-junction. In about 125yds (114m) take waymarked path at driveway to **The Wesleys** to ascend gently. Turn **L** on to tarmac road. Ignore **L** turn but, just 30yds (27m) beyond it, take muddy, narrow path into woodland up on **R**, angled away from road and not signposted. Emerge from trees to trig point on **Walton Hill**. Turn **L**, taking **R-H** of 2 options. Follow this for ¾ mile (1.2km) until just 10yds (9m) beyond National Trust marker post. Here take **R-H** fork to stile. Go steeply down 2 meadows to road beside **Church of St Leonard's** in **Clent**.

❸ Turn **R** then **R** again. At Church View Cottage, opposite church's driveway, turn **L**. In 125yds (114m) take upper, **L** fork. In 90yds (82m), at crossing, go **L**. After further 100yds (91m) ignore options to turn **R** or half **R**. Proceed for further 120yds (110m). Do not climb stile on your **L** but go straight on, soon ascending steeply up wooden steps. After another 100yds (91m) you'll emerge from trees. Now cross track then turn **R**.

❹ Keep on this broad, open path, passing close to (or viewing) a toposcope beside four standing stones. Maintain this line to descend in woodland to road. Just on **L** is car park.

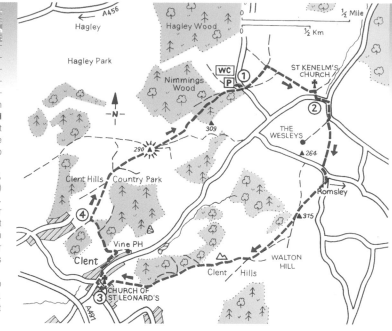

Droitwich Spa Salt into Silver

5¾ miles (9.2km) 2hrs 30min **Ascent:** 230ft (70m) ⚠
Paths: Pavements, field paths, stony tracks, 6 stiles
Suggested map: OS Explorer 204 Worcester & Droitwich Spa
Grid reference: SO 898631
Parking: Long-stay pay-and-display between Heritage Way and Saltway (follow signs for 'Brine Baths')

An historic salt-making town.

❶ From **TIC**, go along Victoria Square. Cross Heritage Way into Ombersley Street East. When it bends keep ahead, passing magistrates' court. After underpass proceed to St Nicholas's Church. Go round churchyard to take another underpass. Turn **L**. Take road over railway to mini-roundabout, filtering **R** to go through 3rd underpass. Walk for 65yds (60m) to fence corner, near lamppost. Turn **L**. In 30yds (27m) turn **R**. At bottom of this cul-de-sac, Westmead Close, turn **L**. Soon take Ledwych Close, on **R**. At **canal** you have left Droitwich Spa.

❷ Turn **L**. At bridge turn **R**; continue. Turn **L** just after A38 bridge. In 110yds (100m) reach **Westwood House** slip road. Facing allotments, take kissing gate to **L**. Beyond woodland go across several fields. Within 500yds (457m) of 2nd driveway is junction.

❸ Turn sharply **R**. Electric fencing leads between paddocks then veer **L** to walk briefly through **Nunnery Wood**. Aim for 2 gateposts beside tree. Keep ahead for ½ mile (800m), beside big **dairy** on **L**, then curving **L** past **industrial estate** to reach Doverdale Lane.

❹ Turn **R** on lane. Just before '30' speed-limit sign, fork **L**. Cross A442. Go through **Hampton Lovett** to **St Mary's Church**. Take meadow path under railway. In 140yds (128m), at footbridge, bear **R**, along field edge. Maintain direction for over ½ mile (800m), walking in trees beside **Highstank Pool** when fence allows. Track leads to evergreens shielding golf tee.

❺ Cross vast field, then aim slightly **L** to metal gate. Follow road under A38 into housing estate. Find path running between Nos 49 and 53. Go through 2 kissing gates flanking level crossing. Turn **L** to pass Gardeners Arms. In 20yds (18m) turn **R** over **River Salwarpe**, into Vines Park. Veer **L** to cross the Droitwich Canal. Over B4090, follow Gurney Lane to High Street – ahead is **Spats Coffee House**. Turn **R**, passing Tower Hill, then **L** into St Andrew's Street.

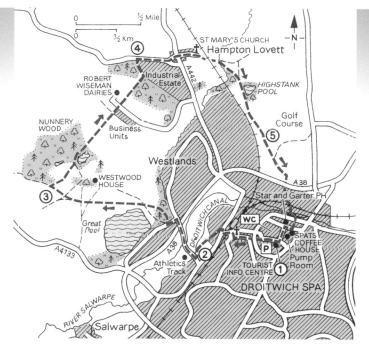

Worcester City Sights and Smells

2½ miles (4km) 1hr 30min **Ascent:** Negligible ⓘ
Paths: City streets and tarmac riverside path
Suggested map: OS Explorer 204 Worcester & Droitwich Spa
Grid reference: SO 846548
Parking: Long-stay pay-and-display car parks at New Road, Tybridge Street and Croft Road

A town walk in Worcester, known for Sir Edward Elgar, its battle, its porcelain, its racecourse and its sauce.

❶ The described route begins at the city side of the road bridge, but you can pick it up anywhere – at The Commandery or the Guildhall, for example – depending on where you have parked. Turn **L**, along North Parade, passing **Old Rectifying House** (wine bar). Turn **R** up **Dolday**, then **L**, in front of **bus station**, along **The Butts**. Turn **L** along **Farrier Street**, **R** into **Castle Street**, reaching northern extremity of route at its junction with Foregate Street.

❷ Go **R** along **Foregate Street**, passing **Shire Hall** and **City Museum and Art Gallery**, continuing along The Cross and into pedestrianised area called **High Street**. Turn **L** into Pump Street. (Elgar's statue stands close to his father's piano shop, at the southern end of High Street.) Turn **L** again, into **The Shambles**. At junction turn **R** into Mealcheapen Street. Another **R**

turn and you are in **New Street** (which later becomes **Friar Street**).

❸ Head down this street (look out for King Charles' House where he stayed during the battle of Worcester in 1651). At end of street is dual carriageway (College Street). Turn **R** then cross carefully, to visit **cathedral**.

❹ Leave cathedral along College Precincts to fortified gateway known as **Edgar Tower**. (It is named after the 10th-century King Edgar, but was actually built in the 14th century. Go through this gateway to see College Green.) Continue, along what is now **Severn Street**, which, unsurprisingly, leads to **River Severn**. Turn **R**, to complete your circuit, by following Kleve Walk, leafy waterside avenue; this section floods at some time most winters, and the **cricket ground** opposite was under several feet of water in 2000. For a more studied insight into the city's rich history, take a guided walk (on weekdays only) with a Green Badge Guide.

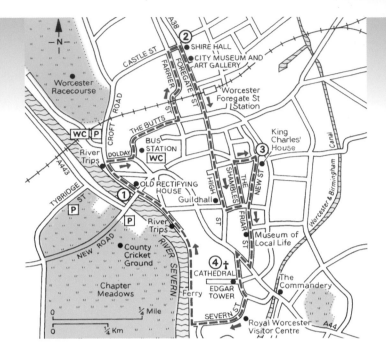

Kingsford Country Park and Villages

5½ miles (8.8km) 2hrs 30min **Ascent:** 410ft (125m) ▲
Paths: Forest rides, meadows, minor roads, village streets, canal tow path, 9 stiles
Suggested map: OS Explorer 218 Wyre Forest & Kidderminster or 219 Wolverhampton & Dudley
Grid reference: SO 835820 (on OS Explorer 218)
Parking: Blakeshall Lane car park, Kingsford Country Park

A backwater that once knew busier times.

❶ Take track inside northern edge of **country park** for 550yds (503m), to point about 50yds (46m) beyond end of extensive garden. To L is wide glade, falling gently; ahead rises woodland track.

❷ Turn **L**, down ride. In 275yds (251m), at 5-way junction, go ahead (not along slight R fork). Join farm track. At road turn **R**, through **Blakeshall**. After 300yds (274m), at R-H bend near power lines, take stile into muddy and brick-strewn field. Keep hedge on your R, following yellow waymarkers into small valley. Reach, but don't go through, 7-bar metal gate before **Debdale Farm**. Turn sharply to **R**, uphill, following vague track. Enter **Gloucester Coppice** at gate and broken stile. Follow this track, soon more defined, all the way to southern end of Blakeshall Lane.

❸ Turn **L**, descending through street, The Holloway, into **Wolverley**. After village stores take 2nd footbridge on **R**. Reach Church of St John the Baptist

by zig-zagging up concreted footpath through deep cutting. Leave churchyard to **L**, by steps. Go down meadow opposite (with fingerpost) to minor road.

❹ Turn **R**. At B4189 turn **L**. In front of **The Lock** pub turn **L**, along tow path. After about 1¼ miles (2km) is Debdale Lock, partly hewn into rock. Some 220yds (201m) further, just before steel wheel factory, is stile.

❺ Turn **L** along track. At T-junction after coniferous avenue turn **R** on broad gravel track. After about 440yds (402m) turn **L** (waymarker), up new wooden steps surfaced with scalpings, into trees. Go up **L-H** edge of one field and centre of another to road. Turn **L** for just 15yds (14m), then **R**. Some 400yds (366m) along this hedged lane take yellow option to **R** (to reduce road walking). At next stile wiggle **L** then **R**. Proceed ahead at junction to road. Turn **R**. In 150yds (137m), walk round wooden barrier to re-enter **country park**. Here, 2 paths run parallel to road – both lead back to car park.

Stourport-on-Severn Hartlebury Common

3¾ miles (5.3km) 1hr 30min **Ascent:** 328ft (100m)

Paths: Tow path, tracks, good paths, some streets
Suggested map: OS Explorer 218 Wyre Forest & Kidderminster or 219 Wolverhampton & Dudley
Grid reference: SO 820704 (on Explorer 218)
Parking: Worcester Road car park on A4025 (poorly signed; height restriction bar spans narrow entrance)

A Georgian 'new town' and a common.

❶ Cross A4025. Turn **L** for 25yds (23m) to take footpath. Strike across bottom part of **Hartlebury Common**: you'll see buildings in far distance. Veer **R**, through silver birches, to find sandy track at back of houses. At housing estate join tarmac briefly, aiming for dirt track beyond 2nd 'Britannia Gardens' sign and in front of Globe House. Shortly turn **L** down tarmac footpath, initially with wooden paling on **L**, to **river**.

❷ Turn **R**. In 650yds (594m) reach lock and Stourport's canal basins. Now, your route is neither across 2-plank walkway at upper lock gate, nor upper brick bridge with timber-and-metal railings; instead take neat brick-paved path to circumnavigate boarded-up **Tontine** public house. Now skirt Upper Basin, passing Severn Valley Boat Centre. Across York Street join tow path. Follow this for just under ¾ mile (1.2km), leaving it at **Bird in Hand** pub, before defunct brick railway bridge.

❸ Go down Holly Road, then half **L** into Mill Road, going under railway then over **River Stour** to B4193. Cross and go to **L** of Myday Windows to take narrow, sandy, uphill path back on to common. Soon, at fork, go **L**, keeping direction as ground levels. Less than 50 paces after joining motor vehicle track reach trig point.

❹ Retrace your 50 paces and go another 30yds (27m), passing waymarker, to junction. Here turn **L**, away from car park. In just 40yds (37m) take **R** fork. In 100yds (91m) take **L** fork (not straight on). At corner of conifer plantation, 275yds further (251m), turn **R**. After 110yds (100m) turn **L**, then in 220yds (201m), just after far end of plantation, enjoy views. Now 65yds (60m) beyond this viewpoint take **R** option at subtle fork. Go forward for another 250yds (229m), until opening. Here step very carefully over pair of exposed and disused (and not actually hazardous) pipes. Follow sandy track slanting downhill for (110yds) 100m, then swing **R**, now head for car park.

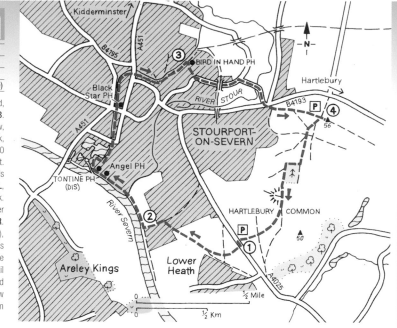

Great Witley Among the Trees

4¾ miles (7.7km) 2hrs 45min **Ascent:** 1,150ft (350m)

Paths: Woodland paths, field paths, tracks, 9 stiles
Suggested map: OS Explorer 204 Worcester & Droitwich Spa
Grid reference: SO 752662
Parking: Car park of Hundred House Hotel (please phone beforehand, tel 01299 896888)
Note: Lots of wild geese on route so please keep dogs under control

A woodland walk up and down some hills.

❶ Cross A451 (take care). Through opening, strike sharply **R**, aiming for hedge end by last house. Step over fence; turn **L** on lane. Walk for ½ mile (800m) soon passing **Walsgrove Farm** and thousands of geese. Don't turn **R** up lane but go half **R**, taking path that becomes avenue of conifers, to top of **Woodbury Hill**. At marker post cross on to narrower track. In 130yds (119m) reach track above **Lippetts Farm**.

❷ Turn **R**, descending. At hairpin bend, aim away from farm to walk along inside edge of wood. Skirt to **L** of buildings at **Birch Berrow**, resuming on service road. As this goes up, **R**, to horse ring, take **R-H** of 2 gates. Go steeply down, taking stile into pines. Very soon, cross stile, turn **R** along road for 100yds (91m), so that you're past **1 Hillside Cottages**, not before it.

❸ Turn **R** again, back uphill. Continue north for nearly 1 mile (1.6km), over several stiles, walking mostly in trees but later enjoying fine views westwards. Then, on top of **Walsgrove Hill**, you'll see the magnificent **clock tower** (1883) of Abberley Hall. Now go steeply down this meadow, to take stile into lane. Turn **R** for 80yds (73m) to B4203.

❹ Cross carefully. Turn **L**, along verge. Take driveway to **Abberley Hall School**. Leave driveway as it swings **R**, keeping this direction close to **clock tower** and all the way, on track, to A443. Take road opposite ('Wynniatts Way') up to brow of hill.

❺ Turn **R**. In about 400yds (366m) reach **trig point**. Walk along ridge path another 650yds (594m) to Worcestershire Way sign at path junction, just beyond which are 4 trees growing in a line across path.

❻ Take path down to **R**, initially quite steeply then contouring as it veers **R**, later descending again. Emerge from woods over stile to walk 2 large fields, meeting road beside **Hundred House Hotel**.

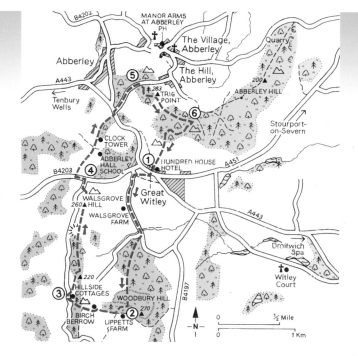

33 | Martley Through the Cider Orchards

6¾ miles (10.9km) 3hrs Ascent: 720ft (219m)

Paths: Field paths, lanes, orchard paths, tracks, river meadows, minor roads, 20 stiles

Suggested map: OS Explorer 204 Worcester & Droitwich Spa

Grid reference: SO 766597 **Parking:** St Peter's Church, Martley

A marvellous, airy stretch of countryside.

❶ Go through churchyard to B4204. Cross to track. In 100yds (91m) enter **school's** grounds briefly then walk in trees, parallel. Turn **R** at stile, then another, to re-enter grounds. Briefly follow **L** edge of playing fields. Another stile gives on to field. At road turn **L**. Turn **R** ('Highfields'). Beside **Lingen Farm** go down track. At bend take stile, across field. Cross stream; ascend, taking **R-H** gates. Reach minor road.

❷ Turn **L**. At **Larkins** go ahead. At **The Peak** walk behind **Ross Green's** gardens. Cross fields to reach road. Go straight over, to partially concealed stile, not diagonally to fingerpost. Walk beside barn, then on, to another lane. Turn **L** to reach fingerpost pointing into apple orchard before **Pear Tree Cottage**.

❸ Follow waymarkers through trees. Emerge at bridge over ditch, beside apple-sorting equipment. Go 220yds (201m) up track, to gap in evergreens. Turn **L**, down orchard ride. At T-junction turn **R**, up to just before gate beside small house. Turn **L**, almost back on yourself. Go through orchard, following faded yellow splodges about 1½ft (45cm) up on tree trunks. Leave by footbridge, crossing fields to B4197.

❹ Turn **R** for 60yds (55m). Take track for ½ mile (800m) to **Rodge Hill's** top. Turn sharp **L**, 'Worcs Way South'. Follow this for 1 mile (1.6km). Steps lead down to road's hairpin bend.

❺ Turn **R**. In 20yds (18m) turn **L**, but in 15yds (14m) turn **R** again, into conifers. Emerge to drop down steeply. At B4204 turn **R** for 200yds (183m). Turn **L**, skirt barn to **L**; go diagonally to **River Teme**. Follow riverside walk, later in **Kingswood Nature Reserve**, for over ½ mile (800m). Leave river when wire fence requires it. Ascend path, later driveway, to road.

❻ Turn **R**, uphill; this soon bends **L**. Near brow move **R** (waymarker) to walk in field, not on road. At end turn **L** but, in 275yds (251m), cross 2 stiles beside caravan. Beside fields and allotments, emerge between **Crown** and garage. Pass telephone box into village. Turn **R** to **church** and start.

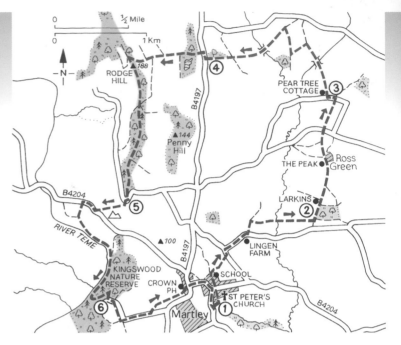

34 | Ravenshill A Wildlife Reserve

2¾ miles (4.4km) 1hr 30min Ascent: 475ft (145m)

Paths: Firm or muddy tracks, meadows, some very short but steep, slippery sections, very little road, 8 stiles. Woodlands and rolling green fields

Suggested map: OS Explorer 204 Worcester & Droitwich Spa

Grid reference: SO 739539 **Parking:** Ravenshill Woodland Reserve (donation)

Elizabeth Barling's woodland dream.

❶ Walk towards **Lulsley** for 150yds (137m). Turn **L** on green track beside Hill Orchard's private drive. Soon in woods, go 500yds (457m), joining another track beside wire enclosures. When stile and nearby gate lead into field on **R**, go 20yds (18m) further. Now go up to **L** on path (you may spot yellow band on branch). In 120yds (110m) climb rustic stile to turn partially **R**. Note well this point, where path joins obliquely from **L**, since you'll be returning this way (junction is easily missed). Go on for 100yds (91m) to driveway. Walk for 30yds (27m) away from house, to follow sign ('bridleway') down to **R**. Soon, at line of laurel bushes, reach tree-lined Worcestershire Way.

❷ Turn **R**. After 650yds (594m) go through gate. Peel **L**, hugging trees but not going under them. A narrow gap would lead into 2nd meadow but on **R** is fenced area. Climb waymarked stile beside padlocked gate. After another gate ascend diagonally **R**, veering **L** as it levels. Maintain this line through metal gates across fields, then wooden gate into woodland. Eventually **The Steps** comes into view. Reach road by descending beside paddock fence, then through more gates, including red one.

❸ Turn **L**. Beyond Threshers Barn and Wain House is Crews Court. Beside fingerpost, go up steps to stile ('Beware butting sheep'). Go ahead, crossing private garden, to paddock. Go ahead but slightly **R**, to padlocked 7-bar gate; climb over this. Now move 20yds (18m) **R** to find your path up – proper stile, rendered obsolete by new fence. Go up quite steeply – you may need to scramble up last bit or find easier part. Now at ridge, don't fall off wobbly stile.

❹ Turn **L**. After 275yds (251m) fork down to **L**, not ahead. At road cross it before turning **R** to walk round bend. Turn **L** along driveway of The Crest then move **L** for Worcestershire Way again. Follow this to Point ❷. Retrace your steps to start.

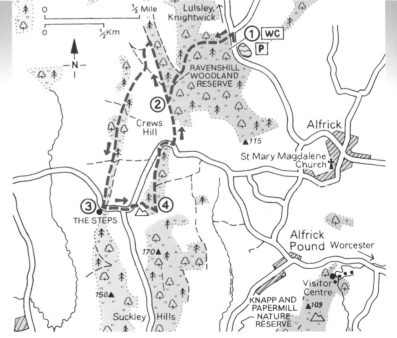

Broadway William Morris

5 miles (8km) 2hrs 30min **Ascent:** 755ft (230m)

Paths: Pasture, rough, tree-root path, pavements, 8 stiles

Suggested map: OS Explorer OL45 The Cotswolds

Grid reference: SP 094374

Parking: Pay-and-display, short stay (4hrs max) in Church Close, Broadway; long stay options signposted

A haunt of the Arts and Crafts pioneer.

❶ Walk down Church Close. Turn **L**. At far end of wall turn **L**, soon passing orchard. At gate before grass turn **R**, to reach bridge over rivulet. Turn half **L**, across pasture. Go to **R-H** field corner. In 40yds (37m) reach bridge beside stone **barn**.

❷ Cross this to waymarker through boggy patch to 2 stiles. Continue to reach gate. Cross field. On joining vague, sunken lane bear **R**, to descend briefly to gate. Tree-lined track reaches 2nd gate within 60yds (55m).

❸ Slant uphill, passing in front of stone building. At woodland turn **L**. Join tarmac road, steadily uphill. At brow turn **L**, into **country park**. Pass **Rookery Barn Restaurant**. Take kissing gate into **Broadway Tower**.

❹ Beyond tower go through gate then take gate immediately on **R**. Move down, **L**, 20yds (18m) to walk in hollow, through pasture. At gate in dry-stone wall. Soon cross track and walk parallel to it in hollow, guided by **Cotswold Way** acorn waymarkers. Aim for gates amongst trees. Beyond, keep ahead. In 45yds (41m), at next marker, bear **R**, walking above road. Soon cross it carefully, to footpath signs opposite.

❺ Leave **Cotswold Way** here. Care is needed in following these next instructions: descend, initially using steps. Ignore path on L after 50yds (46m). After another 50yds (46m) take yellow waymarker pointing up to **R**, over more steps. About 25 paces beyond steps use handrail to descend more steps. After 50yds (46m) run into **Badger Trail** disc. Proceed on this for 10yds (9m). Here orange disc points **L**, but follow low yellow marker ahead. Follow path (beware of exposed tree roots) near top of wood. Eventually take steps on **L**, down to cross road junction.

❻ Take field path ('**Broadway**') through pastures. Swing **L** then **R** under new road. Emerge and turn **R**, on to dead end of Broadway's main street. In centre, 50yds (46m) beyond 3 red telephone boxes, turn **L**, through arcade, to Church Close car park.

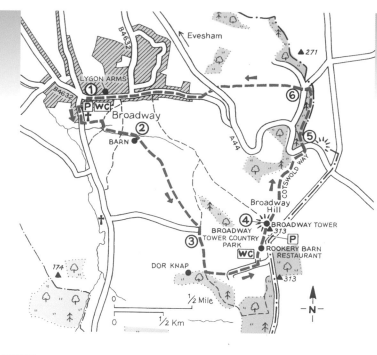

Wellington All Around The Wrekin

8½ miles (13.7km) 3hrs **Ascent:** 1,585ft (485m)

Paths: Woodland footpaths, urban streets, quiet lanes, 2 stiles

Suggested map: OS Explorer 242 Telford, Ironbridge & The Wrekin

Grid reference: SJ 651113

Parking: Belmont or Swimming Pool East car parks, both on Tan Bank, off Victoria Road, Wellington

Note: Rifle range on The Wrekin – warning notices posted, but take care on firing days

A Shropshire classic.

❶ Walk along Tan Bank away from town centre. Cross Victoria Road and continue on Tan Bank then turn **L** on path just after **police station**. Walk to New Church Road; turn **R**. At **Holyhead Road**, turn **L**, then cross to **Limekiln Lane**. Don't miss **Old Hall School** (1480) on corner. Soon you see slopes of **The Wrekin**, as **Limekiln Lane** heads under **M54** into countryside.

❷ At end of lane, go ahead into **Limekiln Wood**; path leads along edge of wood at first. At junction, go to **L**, but few paces further fork **R** into wood. Ignore branching paths, sticking to well-trodden main route. At T-junction by ruined buildings, turn **R**, descend to junction and turn **L**, then **L** again at road.

❸ Turn **R** on access road to **Wrekin Farm**. At **Wenlocks Wood**, leave route. Turn **R** on field-edge path heading towards **The Wrekin**. Cross stile on to its eastern slopes. Continue for a few paces then turn **L**.

❹ Branch **R** where signpost indicates permissive path. Follow this round hill to cross path; turn **R**, to join **Shropshire Way** over summit ridge. Approaching northern end, keep **L** when path forks, then **L** again by prominent beech tree, descending through woods. At edge of woods, leave **Shropshire Way**; turn **R** to lane.

❺ Turn **R** to T-junction, join footpath opposite and go between 2 **reservoirs** before meeting lane; go **L**. When almost level with **Buckatree Lodge**, go ahead into nature reserve. Go ahead along bridleway, past former **quarries** and pool. At junction, ignore path back towards quarries and continue for few paces to find that main track swings **L** and climbs to top of **Ercall**.

❻ As Wellington comes into view, turn **R** on ridge-top path. As you descend, path forks. Go to **R** and join track under M54. Keep ahead along Golf Links Lane to **Holyhead Road**. Cross to footpath opposite. At road (Roseway) turn **R**, then **L** on to Tan Bank

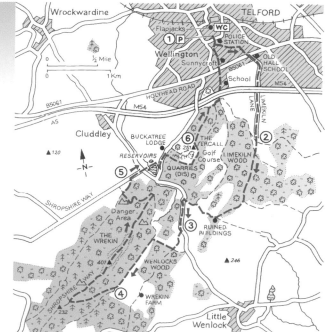

37 Coalport Shropshire's China Town

5 miles (8km) 2hrs **Ascent:** 295ft (90m)

Paths: Mostly excellent, path through Lee Dingle is rough and may be muddy, 1 stile
Suggested map: OS Explorer 242 Telford, Ironbridge & The Wrekin
Grid reference: SJ 677033 **Parking:** Next to Bedlam Furnaces on Waterloo Street, Ironbridge

A superb walk in Ironbridge Gorge.

❶ To **L** of furnaces (as you face them) ascend into parkland, zig-zagging through pergolas and steps. Turn **R** at top, then **L** on Newbridge Road to junction.

❷ Pass to **L** of **Golden Ball Inn**, turn **R** at junction with Jockey Bank, past Victoria Cottage. Go **L** at junction and through gate into wood (**The Crostan**). Stepped path climbs to junction, take **R-H** path, climbing by woodland edge to waymarked junction.

❸ Turn **R** on bridleway, cross 2 meadows and continue through woodland. Fork **L** at 2 junctions; at 2nd bridleway proceed between wood and houses.

❹ Cross stile on **R** into **Lee Dingle** then descend to road. Cross Legges Way, turn **L** under 2 bridges, then **R** on footpath by entrance to **Blists Hill Museum**.

❺ Ignore path L, carry on past wooden posts. Turn **R** on footpath by last post, skirting Blists Hill site, soon entering woodland. Ignore paths L and keep close to museum. When path enters grassland take **L** fork, with trees between path and canal. At junction turn **R**.

❻ Following signs for Coalport, descend to junction by bridge. Turn **L** on **Silkin Way**, then **R** and **R** again past **Shakespeare Inn** and Tunnel Tea Rooms. Cross road bridge, turn **L** over canal and **L** on tow path. Re-cross canal at footbridge, walk past **China Museum**, youth hostel and Slip Room Café. Join High Street and continue, rejoining **Silkin Way** opposite **Brewery Inn**. Follow track to **Coalport Bridge**, cross river.

❼ Turn **R** on Severn Way, go through Preen's Eddy picnic area, climb away from river to continue along old railway trackbed. Turn **R** at signs for **Silkin Way** via **Jackfield Bridge**. Head towards **Ironbridge** past cottages and Maws Craft Centre.

❽ As you approach black-and-white former pub, path leads to access track, bending **L** into woodland. Turn **R** towards **Ironbridge**, soon joining Church Road. Pass **Jackfield Tile Museum** and Calcutts House, carry on at Jackfield Sidings, pass Black Swan. When bridge crosses path, access river. Cross **Jackfield Bridge**, turn **L** past Bird in Hand pub to return to start.

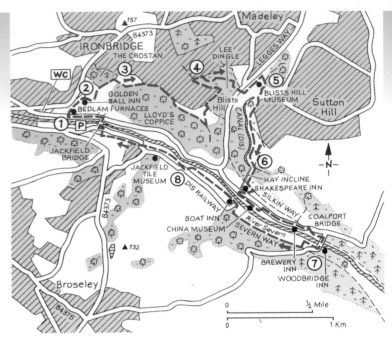

38 Alveley Regeneration Route

5 miles (8km) 2hrs 30min **Ascent:** 425ft (130m)

Paths: Riverside paths, green lanes, can be slippery in places and shallow streams in winter, 12 stiles
Suggested map: OS Explorer 218 Wyre Forest & Kidderminster
Grid reference: SO 753840
Parking: Visitor centre at Severn Valley Country Park, Alveley

A great day out in the Severn Valley.

❶ Walk to river from **visitor centre**, using whichever route you prefer (History Trail, waymarked by red arrows, takes you directly to Miners' Bridge). Don't cross bridge, but descend steps to river bank and walk upstream for nearly 2 miles (3.2km).

❷ Follow short track to car park of **Lion Inn**. Turn **L** past Old Forge Cottage to **Hampton Loade**, then turn **R** past house called The Haywain (just before **River and Rail** pub). Waymarked path leads up through garden into wood, then along edge of field bordering wood. Go along two sides of field to reach top **L** corner, cross stile, turn **R** and cross another stile in next corner. Proceed to track and turn **R**.

❸ After few paces, look for waymarker indicating path on **R**. It descends through woodland to **Lakehouse Dingle**. Pass **former watermill**, cross footbridge and keep going along pebbly track. When you meet concrete track, turn **R** to junction with lane.

❹ Turn left, staying on lane until you've passed **Yewtree Cottage** and its neighbour. Take **L** turn after 2nd cottage. There is no signpost or waymarker here, but it's well-defined field-edge bridleway. At bottom of field look for gap in hedge, where way descends through trees to dingle.

❺ Turn **R**, climb up to meet lane and turn **R** again. After 100yds (91m), join track on **R**. When it bends R, keep straight on instead, along tree-lined green lane. Before long it becomes narrower and deeply rutted as it descends to brook. Cross at stepping stones, or at nearby footbridge. Track then swings **L** beside brook for while before turning sharp **R**.

❻ Turn **L** when you meet lane and walk into **Alveley**. Go through village centre, passing cottages, **church**, pub, shop and bus stop, then turning **R** on footpath next to premises of IGM. Path descends to junction where you turn **L** until you reach field through which well-trodden paths descend to **country park**.

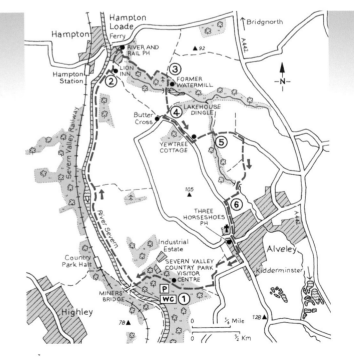

Brown Clee Hills High Hill

7 miles (11.3km) 3hrs 30min **Ascent:** 1,460ft (445m) **3**
Paths: Generally good, but can be very boggy in places, 5 stiles
Suggested map: OS Explorer 217 The Long Mynd & Wenlock Edge
Grid reference: SO 607871
Parking: Cleobury North picnic site, on unclassified road west of Cleobury North

On Brown Clee's upland commons.

1 Cross stile and walk uphill. Intercept path by bench, turn **L**; soon have plantation on **L**, woodland on R. When track forks, go **R** to another track, then **R** again. Soon you're by edge of woodland, with field R.

2 There are 2 houses below and, as you draw level with 2nd, see small clearing on **L**. On edge of it faint path rises diagonally through plantation. It soon becomes clearer and leads to steep straight track. Join this, shortly crossing cattle grid on to pasture.

3 Track turns sharp **L**, leaving tramway incline. Continue to **Abdon Burf**. Stand next to trig pillar (**radio masts** on your R) and look south west to see path descending hill. Follow it down to line of posts. Go through line, keep descending by fence. Path swings **R**, becoming hollow way.

4 Turn **R** at lane, **L** at junction and **L** again at stile. Go along **L-H** edges of meadows, and keep ahead as path merges with remains of old green lane.

5 Approaching **Abdon**, stile leads into garden. Go through, with signs directing you past house and down hollow way to lane. Turn **L** past farm buildings and continue to barns. There's stony track opposite – walk few paces along it to bridleway on **L**. Follow it uphill to **Lane Cottage**.

6 Bear **R** to lane and cross to stile opposite. Go up steep pasture towards fence/hedge on skyline. Cross at stile and continue to top **L** corner of next field. Turn **L** on track, which becomes hollow way at **Highcroft**.

7 Go through gate into pasture and follow **R-H** fence to top corner. Pass through gate and continue to beeches on ridge. Go forward through beeches, straight on along track, which descends through woodland, plantation and bracken to junction. Turn **R**.

8 Where track crosses stream leave it to head downhill, following stream. At track, turn **L**. After 600yds (549m) reach junction. Branch **R** for pub or bus stop at **Burwarton**. If not, keep **L** to start.

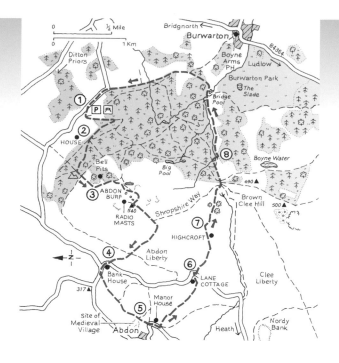

Cleehill The Real Bedlam

8¼ miles (13.3km) 3hrs 30min **Ascent:** 1,330ft (405m) **3**
Paths: Good but rough, uneven and/or boggy in places, 2 stiles
Suggested map: OS Explorer 203 Ludlow
Grid reference: SO 595753
Parking: Car park/picnic site opposite turning for Kremlin Inn on A4117 on eastern edge of Cleehill village

In Shropshires's high and charismatic hills.

1 Walk up track opposite picnic area, towards **Kremlin Inn**. Before you **inn**, go through bridle gate on **L** and along track. After 220yds (201m), right of way to L of it can be difficult – most walkers use track.

2 At **radar station** access road by Hedgehog House, go **R**. Walk to end of **Rouse Boughton Terrace**, go through gate (**L**) to track. Don't follow it but turn **R** along edge of pasture. Go along edge of next field and through gate in corner to **Shropshire Way**, which goes R. Ignore it and keep ahead, cutting corner of field, to meet then follow **L-H** boundary after 300yds (274m).

3 Continue through next field to **L** corner. Follow track to cross **Benson's Brook** at bridge. Climb out of valley on track which passes abutments of old tramway bridge (**Bitterley Incline** is called Titterstone Incline on OS maps), before arriving at **Bedlam**.

4 Turn **L** into hamlet, then fork **R** past Old Shop House and Hullabaloo House towards **Titterstone**

Clee Hill. Gate gives access and path takes you **R**. After passing house, it cuts through bracken.

5 Leave path when reach **Bitterley Incline** again. Climb embankment, joining **Shropshire Way**. Continue uphill towards ruined buildings ahead. Pass to **R** of main **quarry**, then go **L** to top.

6 To north of trig pillar is cairn, **Giant's Chair**. Look north towards Brown Clee Hill to see **Callowgate**, red-roofed farm at edge of moorland. Aim for this, picking best way down slope then across moorland.

7 At **Callowgate**, leave **Shropshire Way** and turn **R** by moorland edge. Joining lane at Cleetongate, turn **R** to **Cleeton St Mary**. Turn **R** past church, **R** past almshouses, **L** on to **Random bridleway** along moorland edge. Keep just to **R** of fence, except where you need to cut corner – obvious when you come to it.

8 When fence makes sharp **L** turn, keep ahead to **radar station** access road. Turn **L** to **Rouse Boughton Terrace** then retrace your steps to start.

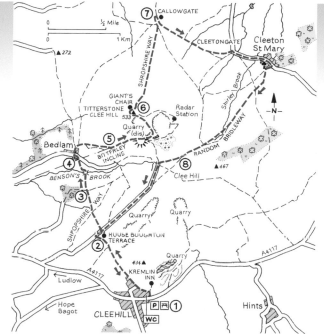

41 Wenlock Edge Close to the Edge

6¼ miles (10.1km) 3hrs **Ascent:** 689ft (210m) ⚠

Paths: Mostly good but ford on Dunstan's Lane can be deep after rain, 10 stiles

Suggested map: OS Explorer 217 The Long Mynd & Wenlock Edge

Grid reference: SO 479875

Parking: Car park/picnic site on east side of unclassified road between Middlehope and Westhope

Along former drovers' roads to Corve Dale.

❶ Turn **L** out of car park along lane. At junction, turn **L** ('Middlehope'). Keep on at next ('Upper Westhope') where road becomes track and bends **L** towards house. Go through gate on **R** instead and along grassy bridleway that enters woodland. Keep straight on at 2 cross paths.

❷ Bridleway emerges into pasture; keep straight on along **L-H** edge to corner. Go through gate and turn **R** on field-edge path, which soon becomes wide track.

❸ Pass cottage and, with barns ahead, look for blue arrows directing sharp **R**. Keep **L** above **Corfton Bache**, deep valley, until blue arrows send you down into valley. Follow it to road at **Corfton** and cross to lane opposite.

❹ As lane degenerates into track, look on **L** for footpath starting at kissing gate. Go diagonally **L** across pasture to prominent stile at far side. Cross farm track and walk to far **R** corner of arable field.

❺ Go through gate, then little way along **L-H** edge of another field until gate gives access to parkland. Follow waymarker. **St Peter's Church** at **Diddlebury** comes into view, providing guide.

❻ Cross 2 stiles at far side of park; descend slope, to **R** of fence. Cross bridge to **Diddlebury**. Turn **R**, then **L** by church. Join footpath: pass to **R** of village hall, then diagonally **R** past **school**, over 2 stiles and across fields to road. Cross to lane; fork **R** after few paces.

❼ Footpath leaves lane on **R**, almost opposite **Chapel Cottage**. Turn **R** to visit **Swan Inn** or continue.

❽ At junction with bridle track by sign ('Aston Top') keep **L** on lane. After ¾ mile (1.2km), branch **L** on byway, **Dunstan's Lane** (no signpost or waymarker). Follow it to Middlehope road; turn **L**. Keep on at Y-junction. When footpath crosses road, turn **L** into woodland. Path is signposted on R, but not L – L branch is few paces further on. Go through woods back to picnic site.

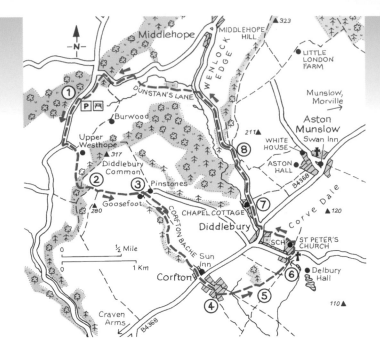

42 Lyth Hill Inspirational Views

8 miles (12.9km) 3hrs **Ascent:** 548ft (167m) ⚠

Paths: Cross-field paths, mostly well-maintained, about 30 stiles

Suggested map: OS Explorer 241 Shrewsbury

Grid reference: SJ 473069

Parking: Car park in country park at top of Lyth Hill: OS map shows bus turning area, not car park

A walk offering panoramic views.

❶ Head south on **Shropshire Way**. Ignore path branching R into Spring Coppice. Way descends to lane; turn **L**, then 1st **R**, on track to **Exfords Green**.

❷ Cross 2 stiles to skirt former **Primitive Methodist chapel**. Leave **Shropshire Way**, going diagonally **R** across field. Cross stile close to far **R** corner and go through copse to lane.

❸ Cross to path almost opposite, following **L-H** field edge. Cross stile into another. Head diagonally across to point near far **R** corner. Cross wobbly stile and continue across another field, past 2 oak trees. Worn path goes obliquely **R** across next 2 fields to lane.

❹ Turn **R**, then **R** again at main road, to pass through **Longden**, and **R** again on School Lane. Descend to cross brook, then go through gate on **L** and diagonally **R** across field corner to stile.

❺ Follow yellow arrow diagonally across next field to stile under oak tree to **L** of telegraph post. Cross another field to road. Path continues opposite, crossing 2 fields to meet lane at **Great Lyth**. Turn **R**, keeping straight on at junction, turn **L** at next.

❻ Turn **R** on access track to **Lower Lythwood Hall** and **Holly Ash**. At latter, turn **L** as track becomes green lane leading to field. Cross field, pass row of 3 oaks, then keep to **R** of pond to reach stile by 2 oaks at far side. In next field go diagonally **R**, then through gate and continue along track for few paces to cross stile on **R**.

❼ Walk straight up sloping field and turn **L** at top. Cross stile in corner and keep on along worn path to waymarker, which directs you **L**, descending beside brook to meet road at **Hook-a-gate**.

❽ Turn **R** for 200yds (183m), **R** again on footpath that climbs to Hanley Lane at **Bayston Hill**. Continue to Overdale Road; turn **R** until you intercept Shropshire Way at Lythwood Road. Turn **R**, following Way to **Lythwood Farm**, across fields to Lyth Hill, and start.

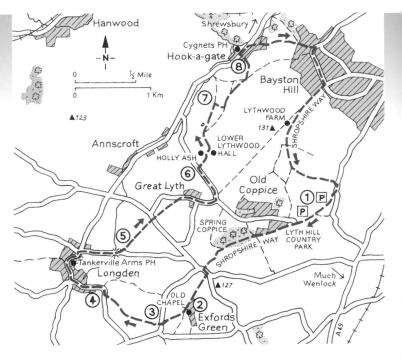

Ellesmere Meres, Mosses and Moraines

7¼ miles (11.7km) 3hrs **Ascent:** 180ft (55m) 🔺

Paths: Field paths and canal tow path, 8 stiles
Suggested map: OS Explorer 241 Shrewsbury
Grid reference: SJ 407344
Parking: Castlefields car park opposite The Mere

A wonderful watery walk.

❶ Cross to **The Mere**; turn **L**. Pass **The Boathouse** and **visitor centre** and walk towards town, until you reach Cremorne Gardens. Join path that runs through trees close by water's edge for ¾ mile (1.2km).

❷ Leave trees for field and turn **L**, signposted 'Welshampton'. Path soon joins track to **Crimps Farm**. Turn **R** past farm buildings to cross stile on **R** of track. Continue along another track.

❸ Track leads into sheep pasture where you go straight on, guided by waymarkers and stiles. When you come to field with trig pillar, waymarker is slightly misleading – ignore it and go straight across. In next field aim for 3 prominent trees close together at far side. As you approach them, turn **L** into field corner.

❹ Go through gate and descend by **R-H** hedge. When it turns corner, go with it, to **R**. Skirt **pool** and keep going in same direction on grassy track, passing another pool. Track soon becomes much better defined and leads to farm where you join road.

❺ Turn **L** and keep ahead at junction into **Welshampton**. Turn **R** on **Lyneal Lane** and follow it to bridge over **Llangollen Canal**. Descend steps to tow path. Turn **R**, passing under bridge. Pass **Lyneal Wharf**, **Cole Mere**, **Yell Wood** and **Blake Mere**, then through **Ellesmere Tunnel**. Beyond this are 3 footpaths signposted 'The Mere'. Take any of these short cuts, but to see bit more of canal, including visitor moorings and **marina**, stay on tow path.

❻ Arriving at **bridge 58**, further choices present themselves. You could extend this walk to include signposted Wharf Circular Walk or to explore town: just follow signs. To return directly to The Mere, however, go up to road and turn **L**.

❼ Fork **R** on road by **Blackwater Cottage**. Turn **R** at top, then soon **L** at Rose Bank, up steps. Walk across earthworks of long-gone **Ellesmere Castle** and follow signs for The Mere or car park.

Whittington From Castle to Canal

6 miles (9.7km) 2hrs 30min **Ascent:** Negligible 🔺

Paths: Tow path, lanes and field paths, very overgrown, 19 stiles
Suggested map: OS Explorer 240 Oswestry
Grid reference: SJ 325312
Parking: Car park next to Whittington Castle – honesty box

Follow the Llangollen branch of the Shroppie through pastoral countryside.

❶ Turn **R** by Shrewsbury road (B5009), using footway on left. After about ½ mile (800m), cross stile and follow waymarked path across 3 fields to far **R** corner of 3rd field.

❷ Walk along edge of next field, with wood on your **L**. Cross stile in corner, then go obliquely across another field as indicated by waymarker. prominent oak tree is useful guide. There is stile near tree, but you may have to wade through nettles to get to it. Continue in same direction across next field to lane and turn **L**.

❸ Keep **L** when you come to fork and continue to **A495**. Turn **R** for few paces, then cross to other side. Join footpath that runs along **L-H** edge of field and footbridge. Beyond these, keep going along field edge until gap in hedge. Go through, but continue in same direction as before, soon going up bank.

❹ Meet canal at **Pollett's Bridge** (No 6). Don't cross it – go under to join tow path. Follow this to **Hindford Bridge** (No 11), then go up to lane. Turn **R** past **Jack Mytton Inn**, then **R** again, signposted 'Iron Mills and Gobowen'.

❺ Take footpath on left. Walk down long, narrow paddock to far end, then cross stile on right. Follow fence to footbridge, then continue across next pasture to another footbridge and keep straight on to stile ahead. Go up to far **R** corner of next field, through gate and then **L** by field edge.

❻ Join track that soon bends **R** beside course of **dismantled railway**. Look out for stile giving access to railway. Turn **R** on former trackbed for few paces, then up bank on **L** – watch out for steps concealed in undergrowth here. Cross stile to far side and cross another stile. Bear **L** to large oak tree, then continue to lane. Follow it to Top Street and turn right, then **L** to **Whittington Castle**.

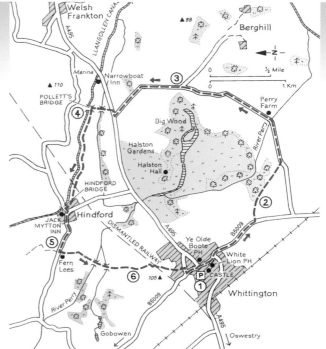

45 Stiperstones Back to Purple

4½ miles (7.2km) 2hrs **Ascent:** 951ft (290m)

Paths: Good paths across pasture, moorland and woodland, 1 stile
Suggested map: OS Explorer 216 Welshpool & Montgomery
Grid reference: SJ 373022
Parking: Car park at Snailbeach

From the mining village of Snailbeach to the dragon's crest of Stiperstones.

1 Take Lordshill lane opposite car park, then join parallel footpath on **L**. Rejoining lane, cross to site of locomotive shed, then continue up lane, noticing green arrows directing you to main sites.

2 Turn **R** on track between **crusher house** and **compressor house**. Few paces past compressor house, turn **L** up steps. At top, turn **R**, then soon **L** up more steps. Turn **L** to Cornish engine house, then **R** and continue through woodland. Short detour leads to smelter **chimney**, otherwise it's uphill all way.

3 Sign indicates that you're entering **Stiperstones National Nature Reserve** (NNR). Woods give way to bracken, broom and bramble before you cross over stile on to open hill. Path climbs slope ahead to stile/gate at top.

4 Two paths are waymarked. Take **L-H** one, which runs between fence and rim of spectacular dingle on

your **R**. Path then climbs away from dingle and meets rutted track. Turn **R**. As path climbs you can see rock tors on summit. There's also one much closer to hand, isolated from rest. This is **Shepherd's Rock**.

5 Just beyond **Shepherd's Rock** is junction marked by cairn. Turn **L** here, then fork **L** to go round other side of rock. Leave NNR at gate/stile. The path runs to **L**, shortly bordered by hawthorn hedge. You'll soon see that this is an old green lane, lined at various points by either hedges/trees on both sides, one line of trees or tumbledown stone wall.

6 At junction take **L-H** path back into NNR. At next junction, fork **R** to leave NNR at gate by plantation. Go diagonally across field to track; turn **R**, going back across field, through plantation, then across pasture on bridleway.

7 Fork **L** at bridleway junction and continue past **Lordshill chapel** to lane. Turn **R** and stay with it as it swings **L** to **Snailbeach**.

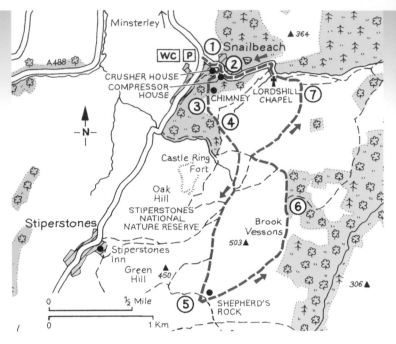

46 The Long Mynd An Ancient Settlement

7½ miles (12.1km) 3hrs **Ascent:** 1,545ft (471m)

Paths: Mostly moorland paths and tracks, 3 stiles
Suggested map: OS Explorer 217 The Long Mynd & Wenlock Edge
Grid reference: SO 453936
Parking: Easthope Road car park, Church Stretton

Prehistoric remains and magnificent views.

1 Walk up Lion Meadow to High Street and turn **R**. Turn **L** at The Square, go past church and straight on into **Rectory Field**. Walk to top **L** corner, turn **R** by edge, soon entering **Old Rectory Wood**. Path descends to junction. Turn **L**, soon crossing Town Brook, then climb again to gate on to **Long Mynd**.

2 Go forward beside brook to railings, continue with brook **L**. After slight height gain, path begins to climb more steeply and heads away from brook. Eventually path and brook meet up again near head of latter.

3 Path crosses brook. Go 50yds (46m) to junction marked by 1st in succession of pink-banded posts. Follow these posts, gaining height gradually again. Ignore branching paths and, after slight rise, you'll see summit ahead on **L**.

4 Meet unfenced road about 100yds (91m) **L** of junction. Turn **L**, ignore path to Little Stretton and go straight on when road bends **L**, joining bridleway. At

next junction, turn **L** to summit, then keep straight on to **Port Way**. Turn **R** past site of Pole Cottage.

5 Turn **L** on footpath, signposted to **Little Stretton**. When wide rutted track forks go **L** – you can see path ahead, cutting green swath over shoulder of **Round Hill**. Go straight on at junction, then descend to **Cross Dyke** (Bronze-Age earthwork). After dyke, path ascends briefly but soon levels out, then descends, eventually following brook to Little Stretton.

6 Cross at footbridge by ford and turn **R** on lane for few paces. Look for footpath on **L**. It climbs by field edge to top corner, then turns **L**, following top of steep slope to pasture. Follow **R-H** edge of this until path enters woodland. Descend to **Ludlow Road**.

7 Here join bridleway next to footpath. It climbs into woodland, emerging at far side to meet track, which becomes road. As it bends **R** there's access **L** to **Rectory Field**. Descend to The Square, turn **R** on High Street and **L** on Lion Meadow to car park.

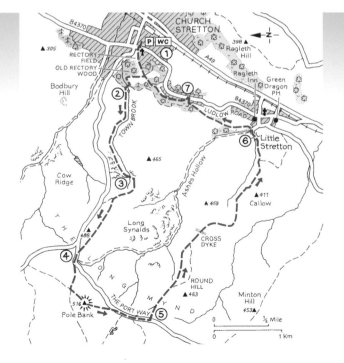

The Strettons The Shapeliest Hills

6 miles (9.7km) 3hrs Ascent: 1,060ft (323m)
Paths: Good paths through pasture and woodland, lane, 14 stiles
Suggested map: OS Explorer 217 The Long Mynd & Wenlock Edge
Grid reference: SO 453936
Parking: Easthope Road car park, Church Stretton

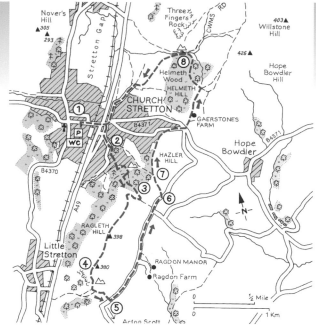

If you like proper pointy hills, the exciting Strettons will make your day.

1 Walk along Easthope Road to Sandford Avenue, turn **R** past station. Cross A49, go along Sandford Avenue, turn **R** on Watling Street South. Turn **L** by postbox, fork **R** on Clive Avenue, and **L** on Ragleth Road.

2 Turn **R** into Woodland Trust reserve, Philla's Grove. Keep **L** at fork, climbing by edge of wood, and **L** at next junction. Leave wood at stile and turn **R** on footpath. After level section, path climbs steeply to stile. Turn **R** for few paces, then fork **L** to higher path, which goes by L-H fence through woodland.

3 When path emerges on hillside, keep ahead to stile, but don't cross it. Turn your back on it and follow path up **Ragleth Hill**, then walk along spine of hill.

4 Pole marks southern summit (smaller of 2), but descent isn't obvious. Go **L**, across rocky area to far fence, then follow it down to corner where stile leads into field. Turn **L** across field corner, cross stile and climb to top **L** corner of next field. Go ahead to far **L** corner of field to lane.

5 Turn **L** on to lane and continue ahead, ignoring **R** turns.

6 Take 2nd path branching off **L** and walk through gorse and bracken to gate. Path continues through woodland.

7 Approaching 2nd gate, don't go through, but turn **R** round **Hazler Hill**. Turn **R** at lane, walk to junction and cross to bridleway opposite, which passes **Gaerstones Farm**. After **Caer Caradoc** comes into view, look for bridleway, **L**, to gate/stile 40yds (37m) away. Descend past **Helmeth Hill** to another bridleway at point where this is crossed by brook.

8 Turn **L**, emerge from woodland into pasture. Continue with fence **L**. Path leads to lane, turn **L** to **Church Stretton**. Turn **R** at Sandford Avenue, cross road, pass station then **L** on Easthope Road to start.

Sunnyhill To Bury Ditches

5½ miles (8.8km) 2hrs Ascent: 804ft (245m)
Paths: Field and woodland paths, one boggy and overgrown, fence and gates to climb; 8 stiles
Suggested map: OS Explorer 216 Welshpool & Montgomery
Grid reference: SO 334839
Parking: Forestry Commission car park at Sunnyhill off minor road north from Clunton

Magnificent views from a dramatic hill fort.

1 From car park, walk back to lane; turn **L**. Descend through hamlet of **Lower Down** and continue to **Brockton**. Turn **L** on track shortly before you come to ford. Pass collection of semi-derelict buses behind **farm**, then go through gate on **L** and walk along R-H edges of three fields, parallel with track.

2 Climb over fence into wood and continue in same direction, contouring round base of **Acton Bank**. After leaving wood path continues through scrub, then through pasture below some old quarries, before it meets lane at hamlet of **Acton**.

3 Turn **L**, pass to **R** of triangular green and join path running past **White House Farm**. Frequent waymarkers guide you past house, across field, then **L** over stile and along R-H edge of another field.

4 Cross footbridge and continue straight across ensuing field towards building at far side. Cross stile in hedge, turn **L** for few paces and then **R** on track which passes by house called **Brookbatch** and rises into woodland. When track eventually bends to **L**, go forward over stile instead and continue climbing.

5 Emerging on to track, turn **L** past **pond**. Cross cattle grid into Forestry Commission property and leave track, turning **R** on footpath leading through beechwoods. It winds through trees to meet **Shropshire Way** (waymarked with buzzard logo). Turn **L**, then soon **R** at junction. Ignoring **R** turn, stay on Shropshire Way, which soon forks **L** off main track.

6 You now have choice of 2 buzzards to follow: main route of Shropshire Way goes straight on, but you should choose alternative route which branches **R**. Path leads to **Bury Ditches** hill fort, then cuts through gap in ramparts and crosses interior. At colour-banded post (red, blue and green), path branches **L** to allow visit to summit, with its toposcope and incredible views. Bear **R** to return to main path and turn **L** to follow it to car park.

49 Offa's Dyke Walking with Offa

8 miles (12.9km) 3hrs **Ascent:** 1,542ft (470m) ▲

Paths: Excellent, mostly across short turf, 8 stiles

Suggested map: OS Explorer 201 Knighton & Presteigne

Grid reference: SO 287734

Parking: Informal parking in Kinsley Wood, accessed by forest road from A488 (or park in Knighton, next to bus station or near Offa's Dyke Centre)

Offa's Dyke on the Welsh border.

❶ Adjacent to car park, at northern end of **Kinsley Wood**, is meadow with barn. Join bridleway which runs along L-H edge of this meadow. After 200yds (183m), veer slightly away from field edge and descend through trees to **Offa's Dyke Path** (ODP).

❷ Turn **R**; follow ODP for 2½ miles (4km). Path runs just above steep slope falling away to west and just below top of **Panpunton Hill**, and follows dyke all way. After climbing around head of combe, it gains top of **Cwm-sanaham Hill** (1,328ft/406m), then continues northwards, soon descending past house, **Brynorgan**.

❸ Meeting road, leave ODP, turning **L**, then **L** again at **Selley Cross**. After ½ mile (800m), just beyond **Selley Hall Cottage**, join footpath on **R**. Follow path to far side of field, then turn **R**, heading to top **R** corner. Cross stile, then continue straight across several fields, to meet lane at **Monaughty Poeth**.

❹ Turn **L** for ¾ mile (1.2km) to junction at **Skyborry Green**. Turn **L**, then immediately **R**, joining bridleway to **Bryney farm**. Turn **R** on footpath (waymarked at regular intervals as it contours round hill), before descending to road again at **Nether Skyborry**.

❺ Turn **L** for ½ mile (800m), then **R** on to ODP just before **Panpwnton farm**. Cross railway and River Teme, then follow Teme towards **Knighton**. Still on path cross border and turn **R** to **Offa's Dyke Centre**.

❻ Leaving **centre**, turn **L** through Knighton, then **L** again on Station Road. After passing **station**, turn **L** on Kinsley Road. Join 1st path on **R** into **Kinsley Wood**, opposite Kinsley Villa and Gillow. Fork **L** after few paces, then embark on almost vertical climb. Gradient eases before path emerges from trees to continue through scrub and across forest road. Keep ahead to top of ridge; turn **L** to walk across summit. Path descends to track. Turn **R** to return to parking area.

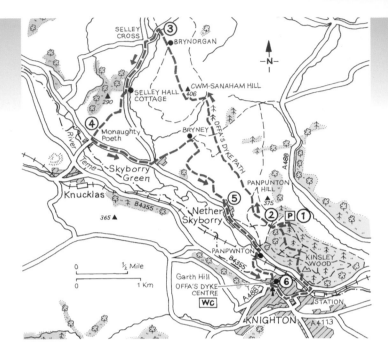

50 Clun Under the Sun

5½ miles (8.8km) 2hrs 30min **Ascent:** 1,066ft (325m) ▲

Paths: Excellent, through mixed farmland (mainly pasture) and woodland, 3 stiles

Suggested map: OS Explorer 201 Knighton & Presteigne

Grid reference: SO 302811

Parking: Car park at Clun community area, signed from High Street

From the tranquil Clun Valley into the hills.

❶ Walk down Hospital Lane to High Street and turn **R** to The Square. Pass **Buffalo Inn**, turn **L** on Buffalo Lane and cross **Clun Bridge**. Go up Church Street, turn **R** on Knighton road, then **L** on Hand Causeway, signposted to **Churchbank** and **Hobarris**.

❷ After ¾ mile (1.2km), take bridleway on **R**, which leaves lane on bend by **Glebe Cottage** and immediately goes **L** into field. Walk up field, through gate at top, then on through 2 more fields to lane running across top of **Clun Hill** (part of prehistoric Clun–Clee Ridgeway).

❸ Path continues opposite, along **R-H** edges of 2 fields. At end of 2nd, go through gate on **R** and diagonally to far corner of another field, then in same direction down next – towards pool in valley below.

❹ Go through gate; turn **L** on byway, then **R** at T-junction. At **Hobarris** go **L** on to track, just before main farm buildings. Soon after crossing brook, branch **L**

along hollow way. When this bends **R**, go straight on, over stile into field. Go straight uphill, joining field-edge track. To your **L**, 3 Scots pines and prehistoric cairn mark summit of **Pen-y-wern Hill**. Turn **L** at lane.

❺ At crossroads, keep ahead, descending to 2nd of 2 bends in lane. Ignore signposted path on **R**; instead take unsignposted path few paces further on. It leads into plantation and soon bends **R**. About 200yds (183m) after this, branch **L** on descending path.

❻ After 200yds (183m) branch **L**, down through oakwood. Continue to meet path at bottom of wood.

❼ Turn **L** on path, which almost immediately swings **L**, back into wood and winds through trees to meet lane. Turn **R** towards **Clun**.

❽ Turn **L** at junction with 2 tracks. Keep along lane until stile on **R** gives access to field. Go diagonally **L** towards Clun. Join lane, then turn **R** and cross footbridge by ford. Turn **R** to High Street and Hospital Lane.

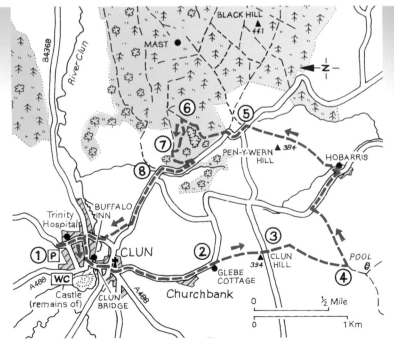

Cornwell To Churchill

5½ miles (8.8km) 2hrs 30min Ascent: 459ft (140m) ⚠️
Paths: Open farmland, village lanes, quiet roads, 12 stiles
Suggested map: OS Explorer OL45 The Cotswolds
Grid reference: SP 270270
Parking: Lay-by beside phone box at Cornwell

A walk linking two intriguing villages.

❶ Turn **L**. Walk down and up through **Cornwell**. Pass farm, **R**. Turn **R** ('D'Arcy Dalton Way'). Where track veers **L**, continue, by fingerpost. Walk down orchard; bear **L**. Go **R** at corner through hedge. Soon go through gate on **L**. Turn **R** and walk downhill. Cross stile, **R**; follow path down towards **St Peter's Church**.

❷ Go through gate into churchyard. Pass church, and leave via gate. Walk down hill, cross bridge at bottom and go up to gate. Turn **R** along drive, passing **Cornwell Glebe**. Bear **L**. Pass turning to Salford.

❸ Turn **R** along bridleway ('Kingham'). Follow this for ½ mile (800m); cross stile on **L**. Continue down field edge. Cross footbridge. Follow path diagonally **R**. Cross footbridge. Bear **R** along stream. Soon bear **L** and cross stile. Cross track. Cross footbridge opposite. Bear diagonally **R** up field. Cross footbridge in hedge. Maintain direction through another hedge.

❹ Cross stile into woods. Follow path down, over footbridge and up other side. Go through gate and ahead towards **Churchill**. Cross stile. Bear **R** beside house. Cross stile. Turn **L** up road. Pass post-box; turn **R** along path. At next road turn **L**. At top turn **R**.

❺ Turn **R** before **church**. Follow path round back of pub. Cross stile, pass barn and maintain direction into field. Soon turn **R** over stile and along lane. When you reach road turn **L**. Turn **R** at next junction, then **L** at end. Follow road out of village, passing old **chapel**. Continue through **Sarsden Halt**.

❻ Follow road **R**, then keep ahead along green lane. After ½ mile (800m) climb stile on **L**; bear diagonally up field. Walk up hedge and turn **R** along road.

❼ Continue through **Kingham Hill Farm**. Pass through gate at other side and across 2 fields. Cross stile, then footbridge and stile; keep ahead. Pass gate and continue up field. Cross another stile and continue, bearing slightly **L** over hillcrest. Take gate to **L** of main gate. Turn **L** up road to return to your car.

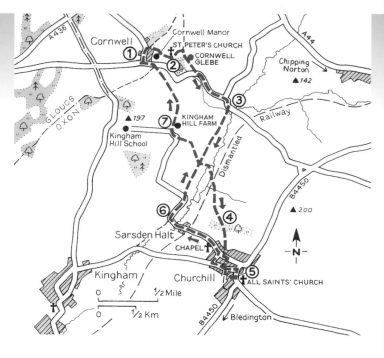

Chipping Norton The Rollright Stones

8 miles (12.9km) 4hrs Ascent: 295ft (90m) ⚠️
Paths: Field paths and tracks, country roads, 9 stiles
Suggested map: OS Explorer 191 Banbury, Bicester & Chipping Norton
Grid reference: SP 312270
Parking: Free car park off A44, in centre of Chipping Norton

An ancient and mythical site.

❶ Follow A44 downhill. Pass Penhurst School, then veer **R**, through kissing gate. Skirt **L-H** edge of recreation ground and aim for gate. Descend to bridge and, when path forks, keep **R**. Go up slope to 3 stiles and keep ahead along **R** edge of field. Make for gate and drop down to double gates in corner.

❷ Cross track just beyond stile. Walk towards **Salford**, keeping hedge **L**. Continue into village. Turn **R** by patch of grass ('Trout Lakes – Rectory Farm').

❸ Follow track to **R-H** bend. Go ahead here, following field edge. Make for gate ahead. Turn **R** in next field. About 100yds (91m) before field corner, turn **L**. Follow path across to opening in boundary. Veer **L**, then **R** to skirt field. Cross stream. Maintain direction in next field to reach road.

❹ Turn **L**, then **L** again for **Little Rollright**. Visit **church** then retrace route to D'Arcy Dalton Way on **L**. Follow path up field slope to road. Cross over.

Continue between fields. Head for trees and approach stile. Don't cross it; instead, turn **L** and skirt field, passing close to **Whispering Knights**.

❺ At road, turn **L** to visit **Rollright Stones**. Return to Whispering Knights, head down field to stile and cross it to another. Continue along grassy path. Turn **R** at stile towards **Brighthill Farm**. Pass beside buildings to stile. Head diagonally **R** down field to further stile. Keep boundary on **R** and head for stile in bottom **R** corner of field. Make for bottom **R** corner of next field. Go through gate and skirt field; turn **L** at road.

❻ Keep **R** at fork and head towards **Over Norton**. Walk through village to T-junction. Turn **R**. When road swings to **L** by Cleeves Corner, join track ('Salford'). When hedges gives way, look for waymark on **L**. Follow path down slope, make for 2 kissing gates; follow path alongside wall to reach **church**. Join Church Lane. Follow it as far as T-junction. Turn **R** and return to town centre.

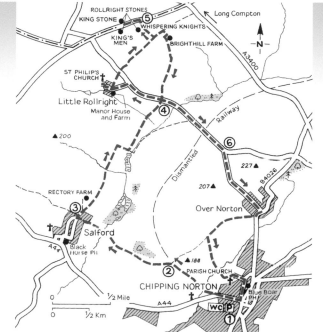

53 Burford A Classic Cotswold Town

5 miles (8km) 2hrs 30min **Ascent:** 250ft (76m) ▲

Paths: Field and riverside paths, tracks, country roads, 7 stiles

Suggested map: OS Explorer OL45 The Cotswolds

Grid reference: SP 252123

Parking: Large car park to east of Windrush, near parish church

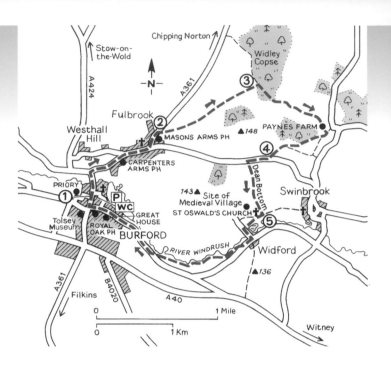

Discover the delights of an ancient settlement with a long history on this attractive walk through the Windrush Valley.

❶ Head north along High Street to **Windrush**. Cross over river and turn **R** at mini-roundabout towards **Fulbrook**. Pass **Carpenters Arms** and continue along road. Avoid turning for Swinbrook and pass **Masons Arms**. Keep ahead, passing Upper End on **L**, and look for footpath on **R** by Masons Arms sign.

❷ Follow steps cut into side of slope up to field edge and then swing **R**. Follow boundary to waymark just before slope and curve **L** to cross field. Go through gap in hedge on far side and cross field to opening in hedgerow. Cross next field towards curtain of woodland and make for track.

❸ Keep **R** and follow track through woodland. Break cover from trees and pass row of cottages. Continue down track to **Paynes Farm** and, just beyond it, turn **R** to join signposted right of way. Head for gate and follow unfenced track towards trees. Descend slope to gate and continue ahead between hedges up hill to road.

❹ Turn **R** and follow road down into dip. Swing **L** at stone stile and sign for **Widford** and follow grassy ride through verdant **Dean Bottom**. Make for stile, turn **R** when you reach T-junction and visit Widford's **St Oswald's Church.**

❺ On leaving church, veer **R** and follow grassy track, passing lake on **L**. Turn **L** at road, recross Windrush and turn **R** at junction. Keep to road until you reach footpath sign and stile on **R**. Follow riverside path across series of stiles, to eventually reach road. Turn **R** towards **Burford**, pass **Great House** and **Royal Oak** and return to High Street. Leave plenty of time either at the start or finish of the walk to explore Burford. Take a leisurely stroll through the town and you'll stumble across a host of treasures – especially in the little roads leading off the High Street.

54 Minster Lovell A Domesday Village

4 miles (6.4km) 1hr 30min **Ascent:** 180ft (55m) ▲

Paths: Meadows, tracks, pavement and lane, woodland, 17 stiles

Suggested map: OS Explorer 180 Oxford, Witney & Woodstock

Grid reference: SP 321114

Parking: Car park (free) at eastern end of Minster Lovell, above church and hall

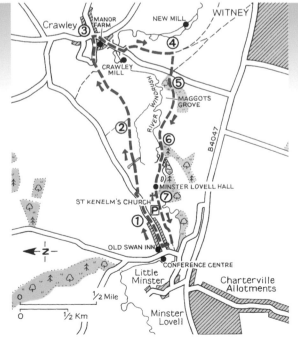

A gentle stroll through meadows and woods beside the Windrush.

❶ Walk up lane ('Crawley'). At end of village cross stile, **R**. Take footpath diagonally **L** across field ('Crawley'). Cross stile and keep ahead along path, with stone wall to **L**. Mill chimney on horizon belongs to **Crawley Mill**.

❷ Cross stile and ahead up slight incline. Cross another stile, go through gate and continue on path, walking up green tunnel of lane. Pass above **Crawley Mill**. At road turn **R**. Follow this down into **Crawley**. At bottom, Lamb Inn is on **L**.

❸ Turn **R**. Follow pavement past **Manor Farm**, with its huge pond. Cross humpback bridge over **Windrush**. At other side of bridge cross road. Turn **L** through gate ('Witney'). Follow bridleway beside stream, marked by line of willows.

❹ At junction of paths by gate look ahead and **L** to see **New Mill**. Turn **R** through gate and walk up field edge. Pass gate and cross road. Climb stile, go straight on to 2nd stile, and follow path down through woods.

❺ At bottom cross stile and follow path along fence. Wildflower meadows of **Maggots Grove** lie to **R**. Continue over 3 more stiles and bear **L** beside trees. Cross stile by meander of river.

❻ Cross further stile and enter woods. At gate bear **R**, following arrows, and cross 2 footbridges. After short distance cross bridge over river. Go through squeeze gate towards **Minster Lovell Hall**. Climb stile and go through gate to explore ruins.

❼ Leave by top entrance and walk through **churchyard**. Cross slab stile, continue along grassy path with village up to your **R**. Cross footbridge and stile and veer to **R**. Cross 1 stile then another into Wash Meadow recreation ground. Keep **R** and go through gate on to high street, with **Old Swan** pub to **L**. Turn **R**. Walk through village to car park.

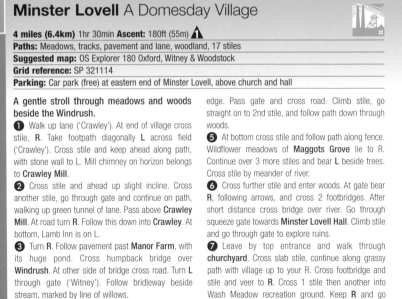

Broughton A Moated Castle

2¾ miles (4.4km) 1hr 30min **Ascent:** 82ft (25m)

Paths: Field and parkland paths and tracks, some roads, 6 stiles

Suggested map: OS Explorer 191 Banbury, Bicester & Chipping Norton

Grid reference: SP 421384

Parking: Limited spaces in Broughton village

To a splendid Tudor pile.

❶ Keep **Wykeham Lane** R and parkland L and walk through **Broughton**. Pass Danvers Road on R-H side, followed by **Danvers Cottage** on L. When road curves R just beyond cottage, swing **L** over stile ('North Newington'). Keep ahead across field to reach stile in next boundary, then continue in next field to cross footbridge in trees (maybe obscured by foliage during summer). Continue ahead, keeping line of trees on your R-H side and, three-quarters of way along field boundary, look for footbridge on **R**.

❷ Cross footbridge, followed by concrete track, to reach stile. Head diagonally **R** across field to road. Take right of way on opposite side and follow stretch of **Macmillan Way** between fields to reach stile. Cross stile to lane; turn **L**. Walk towards **North Newington**, passing entrance to **Park Farm** on your R-H side. Pass **Blinking Owl** pub and Wheelwright Cottage then turn **L** into The Pound, opposite old village pump.

❸ Walk past **Pound Cottage** and look for footpath which starts about 30yds (27m) beyond it on R-H side. Follow footpath diagonally **R** across field to reach wide, obvious gap in hedgerow on far side. Turn **L** to reach another gap in hedge, then head obliquely **R** in field, making for top corner, which is defined by trees and hedgerow. Pass through gate and keep ahead, with field boundary on your immediate **L**. Walk along to next gate and then down field to road.

❹ Cross road to galvanised gate and follow track towards **barns**. Keep to **L** of barns and look for stile and footpath branching off to **L**, running hard by fence on R-H side. Follow path to reach stile in far boundary and cross over into parkland of **Broughton Castle**. Soon **Broughton** church spire and castle come into sight ahead. Continue across parkland and down to meet castle drive. Head for gate into churchyard then follow path to reach **B4035** on outskirts of **Broughton**. Turn **L** along road and return to start.

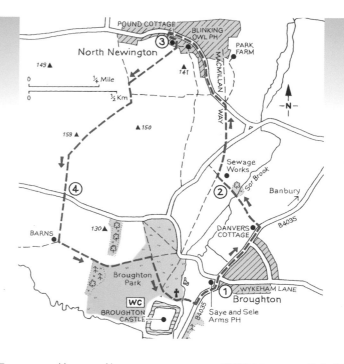

Hook Norton A Towering Success

4½ miles (7.2km) 2hrs **Ascent:** 164ft (50m)

Paths: Field paths, tracks and bridleways, quiet roads

Suggested map: OS Explorer 191 Banbury, Bicester & Chipping Norton

Grid reference: SP 355330

Parking: Spaces in Hook Norton village centre

Explore delightful ironstone country before visiting Hook Norton Brewery.

❶ With **church** on your L, turn **R** into Middle Hill. Follow it down to next road and keep ahead to bridge. Turn **L** into Park Road and follow it to next junction. Continue ahead, keeping row of bungalows on L. When road bends sharp L, join waymarked bridleway and follow it out of Hook Norton. Pass remains of old **railway viaduct** and walk along to **Park Farm**.

❷ Cross cattle grid and continue for about 50yds (46m). When track forks, keep **L** and follow path to gate. Continue along field edge to next gate and follow obvious track as it curves to **R**. Cross ford at footbridge and make for next gate. Follow field boundary and cross into next field, keeping trees and hedgerow on L. Head for galvanised gate and swing **R** at bridleway sign. Head diagonally across field and look for gate in trees in top boundary. Follow grassy path alongside fence to reach drive.

❸ Turn **R** here, away from **Cradle Farm**, and walk along to outbuildings at point where drive bends sharp L. Keep **R** here and follow track alongside pair of semi-detached **houses** on R. Emerge from trees to 3 tracks; take middle track up slope between fences to reach road. Cross over to galvanised gate and follow bridleway between fences, trees and paddocks. On reaching gate turn **R** to wrought iron gate leading into field. Turn **L** and make for further gate into next field. Pass to R-H side of fencing and make for gate in field boundary.

❹ Turn **R** to join avenue of lime trees. At length, drive reaches road. Turn **L** then take 1st **R** for **Hook Norton**. At 1st junction, turn **R** at sign for Swerford and walk along to **Hook Norton Cutting**. Retrace your steps to junction and continue ahead towards Hook Norton. Pass speed restriction sign and keep ahead into village. Pass Park Road on R and take Middle Hill back up to church and pubs.

57 Great Tew A Rare Plot

4 miles (6.4km) 1hr 45min **Ascent:** 150ft (46m)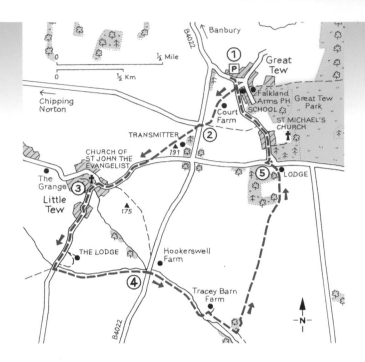
Paths: Field paths and tracks, stretches of quiet road, 3 stiles
Suggested map: OS Explorer 191 Banbury, Bicester & Chipping Norton
Grid reference: SP 395293
Parking: Free car park in Great Tew

A lovely village and undulating countryside.

❶ From car park turn **L**, pass turning to Great Tew, follow road as it bends **R** and as it straightens out turn **R** at footpath sign ('Little Tew'). Go diagonally across field, heading for farm outbuildings on brow of hill. Cross stile in front of them to gate and stile and keep field boundary on **R**. Follow it along to pair of galvanised gates and stile leading out to road at junction.

❷ Cross over and take path ('Little Tew'). Head diagonally across field, passing to **R** of **transmitter**. On reaching road, turn **R** and walk down hill into **Little Tew**. Pass through village and turn **L** at turning for Enstone. On corner is **Church of St John the Evangelist**.

❸ Follow road out of Little Tew and look for entrance to **The Lodge** on L. Continue for few paces to some white railings, then turn immediately **L** at opening in hedge leading into field. Keep along **L** boundary and make for galvanised gate in field corner. Continue ahead on grassy path, passing house over on L. Keep ahead on clear track to kissing gate leading out to road.

❹ Cross over and follow track ('Sandford'). Keep alongside trees and then round to **L** towards house. As you approach it, turn **R** and join another track heading southeast. Keep fence on R and make for gate by trees. Continue for few paces to gate and waymark on **L**. Take path, keeping belt of woodland and field edge on your L. Beyond some trees, continue ahead into next field, again beside tongue of woodland. Pass into next field and continue alongside trees. Approach **lodge** and keep to L of it.

❺ Follow drive to meet road, cross over to junction and take turning ('Great Tew'). Pass entrance to **St Michael's Church** (a fine medieval church) on R. Look for village **school**, also on R, and then, just beyond turning to **Great Tew**, return to car park.

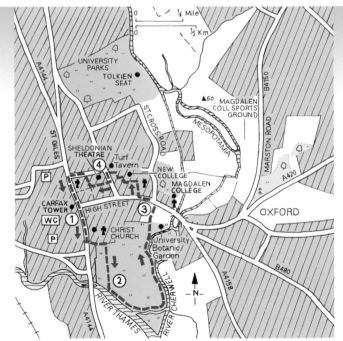

58 Oxford Heavenly Jerusalem

2¼ miles (3.6km) 1hr 15min **Ascent:** Negligible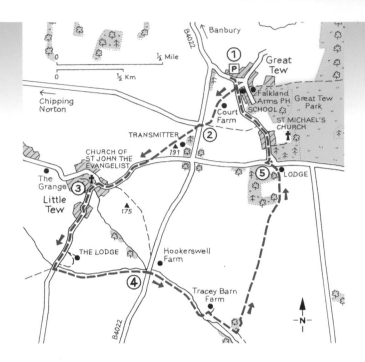
Paths: Pavements, field and riverside paths, 2 stiles
Suggested map: OS Explorer 180 Oxford
Grid reference: SP 513062
Parking: Parking in city centre, or use park-and-ride, or travel by train

Discover Oxford's quiet corners and hidden backwaters.

❶ Start at **Carfax**, where 4 streets converge. Charles II was proclaimed King at **Carfax Tower** in 1660. Walk ahead into St Aldates and head for entrance to **Christ Church**, Oxford's largest college, founded in 1525 by Cardinal Wolsey. When he was disgraced it was refounded as King Henry VIII's College. Later it became known as **Christ Church** when the college and the cathedral became one. Leave by south exit and walk ahead down tree-lined New Walk. On L is Christ Church Meadow.

❷ On reaching **Thames** tow path, swing **L** and follow river bank. Keep ahead until you reach confluence of Thames and **River Cherwell**. Avoid steeply arched footbridge and keep alongside Cherwell. River meanders between meadows and sports fields. Leave river bank and pass through wrought-iron gates to walk up Rose Lane.

❸ With Magdalen Bridge and **Magdalen College** bell tower on your R, turn **L** at **High Street** or 'the High', as it is known in Oxford. Cross Longwall Street and turn R into Queen's Lane. Continue into New College Lane and on **R**, beyond arch, is entrance to **New College**. Keep along New College Lane to Bridge of Sighs, a 1913 replica of its Venice namesake, and ahead of you now is **Sheldonian Theatre**, designed by Sir Christopher Wren and completed in 1669.

❹ Turn **L** here for Radcliffe Camera and cross Radcliffe Square towards Brasenose College, which probably took its name from a door-knocker in the shape of a nose. Turn **R** into Brasenose Lane, then **R** again into Turl Street, cutting between Jesus College and Exeter College. Make for Broad Street and on R is St Giles, where Charles I drilled his men during the Civil War. Turn **L** into Cornmarket Street, passing Church of St Michael at North Gate. Its Saxon tower is the oldest building in Oxford. Return to **Carfax**.

Blenheim Palace A Sweet House

7 miles (11.3km) 3hrs Ascent: 150ft (46m) ⚠

Paths: Field paths and tracks, parkland paths and estate drives. Some quiet road walking, 3 stiles

Suggested map: OS Explorer 180 Oxford

Grid reference: SP 411158

Parking: Spaces in centre of Combe

To one of Britain's top country houses.

❶ From village green, take road ('East End'). Swing **R** by village pump into churchyard and keep to **L** of **church**. Exit through gap in boundary wall, flanked by 2 gravestones, and begin skirting **R-H** edge of sports field. After 50yds (46m), branch off into trees, then head diagonally across field. Cross into next field and keep to **R** edge of wood. In next field, turn **L**, still with trees **L**, and go up slope to woodland corner. Pass through gap in hedge; cross field.

❷ Exit to road, turn **L** and keep **R** at next junction. Walk to **Combe Gate**. Go through kissing gate into **Blenheim Palace** grounds, keep **L** at junction; follow drive through parkland. As it sweeps **L** to cattle grid, veer off to **R** by sign ('visitors are welcome to walk in the park'). Follow path to stile. Keep **R** when path divides and walk beside western arm of **The Lake**.

❸ Eventually reach tarmac drive. Turn **R** and walk towards **Grand Bridge**. As you approach it, turn sharp

L, passing between mature trees with **Queen Pool** on **R**. Cross over cattle grid and keep ahead through park. With **Column of Victory** on your **L**, follow drive as it sweeps to **R**.

❹ Turn **L** at cattle grid, in line with buildings of Furze Platt on **R**. Join **Oxfordshire Way**, cross stile and follow grassy track alongside trees, then between fields. At length cross track and continue towards woodland. Enter trees and turn **L** after few paces to join clear track running through wood.

❺ After 150yds (137m) take 1st **L** turning, crossing footbridge to reach edge of field. Keep **R** here, following obvious path across fields. When you reach track, turn **R**. Keep alongside trees to junction. Turn **R** and follow track down through wood and diagonally **L** across strip of pasture to opening in trees. Go up to track; cross it to ladder stile.

❻ Turn **L** to hedge; turn **R**, keeping it and ditch on **R**. Skirt field to road, turn **R** and walk into **Combe**.

Bladon Churchill's Grave

5 miles (8km) 2hrs 15min Ascent: 90ft (27m) ⚠

Paths: Field and woodland paths and tracks, quiet roads, 7 stiles

Suggested map: OS Explorer 180 Oxford

Grid reference: SP 468138

Parking: Limited spaces outside Begbroke church, St Michael's Lane

The final resting place of Winston Churchill.

❶ Keep **church** behind you, walk to Spring Hill Road. Turn **R**. Follow lane through 2 sharp bends, passing **Hall Farm**. Avoid path on **R**; continue to stile and galvanised gates. Follow track up gentle slope to next stile and cattle grid. Keep ahead, passing house on **L**, then swing **R** across field, passing under telegraph wires. Pass into next field; turn **R**.

❷ Follow obvious boundary across several fields, eventually turning **L** in corner. Continue for 50yds (46m) and look for stile and footbridge on **R**. Continue in next field, with hedge on **L**. At field corner, continue for few paces; turn **R** through opening in hedge into adjoining field. Maintain direction, with boundary **L**. Make for stile and oak in field corner. Continue across next field, keeping to **L** edge of woodland. With trees by you on **R**, follow path towards **Burleigh Lodge**. Swing **L** for few paces to stile leading out to road.

❸ Turn **R** by millennium stone, pass lodge and walk

to footpath sign on **R** ('Bladon'). Cross stile and keep hedge on **L**. Make for footbridge in field corner, turn **L** and follow hedgerow. Look for hedge running diagonally **R**; keep it **L** and head towards Bladon. Make for stile on to road on bend. Go forward, keep entrance to **Lamb** pub car park on **L**, continue to next junction; cross to Church Street. Walk to **Church of St Martin**; head through churchyard to gate on far side.

❹ Turn **R**; follow tarmac lane to wooden gates. Continue on field path to corner; turn **R** at waymark. With hedgerow **L**, pass to **L** of woodland and head for white gate, with road beyond. Turn **L** by lock-up garages and follow path ('Begbroke').

❺ Cross rectangular pasture and, at far end, follow path into trees and through gate. Emerge at length from wood at another gate and continue ahead along field boundary towards **Begbroke**. Go through gate in corner; follow path alongside drive to road. Turn **L** and **L** again into St Michael's Lane, returning to church.

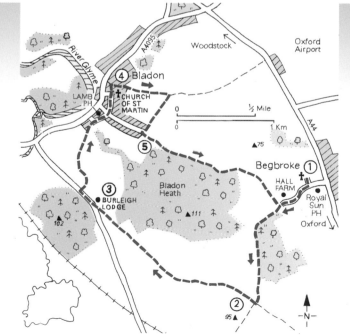

61

Garsington Agriculture and Aristocracy

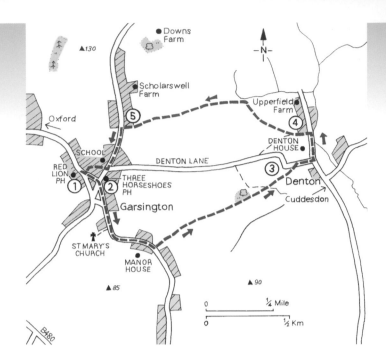

3 miles (4.8km) 1hr 15min Ascent: 165ft (50m)
Paths: Field paths and roads (can be busy in Garsington), 11 stiles
Suggested map: OS Explorer 180 Oxford
Grid reference: SP 580024
Parking: Spaces near Red Lion in Garsington village

Pass a manor house, which was once used as a sanctuary by some of Britain's most famous writers and artists, including Virginia Woolf and Bertrand Russell.

❶ Facing **Red Lion**, turn **L** and walk through **Garsington**. Veer half **L** at The Hill, leading to Sadlers Croft. Keep **R** and climb bank to bollards by war memorial. Cross over to The Green, keeping **Three Horseshoes** on L and historic cross on R.

❷ Continue along road to **St Mary's Church** and pass **Manor House**. Keep on road and, just as it descends quite steeply, branch **L** at sign ('Denton'). Strike out across field and pass between 2 trees. Ahead on horizon is hilltop church at Cuddesdon, with trees behind. Make for gap in boundary and continue in next field. Look for waymark in wide gap in next boundary and aim to **R** of copse. Pass through gap in field corner, avoid path on L and head diagonally **L** across field to far corner. Cross 2 stiles to reach road.

❸ Turn **R** and pass alongside stone wall on L. Walk along to R-H bend and bear **L** at sign ('Brookside only'). **Denton House** is on L and dovecote can be seen on R. Pass stile and footpath on R and keep along lane for few paces, turning **L** at public footpath.

❹ Head for stile and pass ornamental wall enclosing Denton House. Cross over paddock to next stile then go diagonally **R** across field to stile. Then head diagonally **L** in next field, keeping **farm** over to R. Cross 2 stiles and begin approaching houses of Garsington. Make for stile in **R-H** corner of field, keeping boundary on R in next pasture. Climb gently and look for stile on **R**. Cross it, turn **L** and make for 2 stiles in field corner. Join drive and follow it up to road.

❺ Turn **L** towards **Garsington**, pass houses of North Manor Estate and primary **school** before turning **R**, opposite **Denton Lane**, to join footpath. Follow lane, keep **R** and make for road. Turn **R** and return to parking area by **Red Lion**.

62

Watlington A Civil War Battlefield

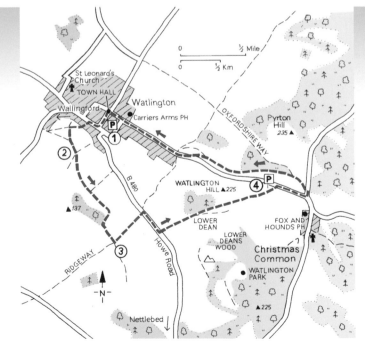

5½ miles (8.8km) 2hrs Ascent: 200ft (60m)
Paths: Field paths and tracks, stretches of road (busy), 9 stiles
Suggested map: OS Explorer 171 Chiltern Hills West
Grid reference: SU 690943
Parking: Town car park in Watlington

From a quaint small town climb into spectacular Chiltern country and enjoy views towards a famous battleground, where Royalist and Parliamentarian armies engaged in bitter conflict.

❶ Turn **L** out of car park towards town centre. Turn **L** at junction, by **Town Hall**, and follow Couching Street to junction with Brook Street. Turn **R** and walk along to No 23. Take footpath opposite and follow it between walls. Make for kissing gate, keep **R** at immediate fork and cross field. Keep to **L** of tree and head for 2nd kissing gate. Veer **L** at fork and cut between trees and fencing.

❷ Turn **L** at track and follow it round to **R**. Swing **L** at 'private – no access' sign. Further on, follow path round to **R** and make for junction with concrete farm track. As you reach it, turn **L** to join path running along field edge. Keep hedge and trees on R and follow it along to stile in corner.

❸ Turn **L** here and walk along **Ridgeway** to road. Turn **R** towards Nettlebed and then take 1st **L** turning. Follow track for about 70yds (64m) and, when it forks at wooden post-and-brick pillar, keep **L** and follow enclosed path through trees to 2 stiles. Continue on path, climbing gently to kissing gate. Keep **L** at fork and keep climbing. Break cover from trees and then enter woodland again. Go through kissing gate and pass between beech trees to next gate. Follow path to **R** of **Watlington Hill** car park and turn **R** at road.

❹ Head for **Christmas Common** and turn **L** at next junction. Follow road for about 50yds (46m) and turn **L** at **Oxfordshire Way** sign. Cross stile and keep along field perimeter to 2nd stile. Keep ahead for about 70yds (64m) to stile and leave Oxfordshire Way at this point. Follow sunken path, looking for white arrows on trees, and descend gradually to fork. Keep **L** alongside chalk pit, go through kissing gate and turn **R** at road. Follow it back to car park.

Uffington The White Horse

7 miles (11.3km) 3hrs **Ascent:** 415ft (126m)

Paths: Ancient tracks and field paths, road (can be busy), 13 stiles
Suggested map: OS Explorer 170 Abingdon, Wantage
Grid reference: SU 293865
Parking: Large free car park near Uffington White Horse

Legends and magic on this downlands walk.

❶ From car park go through gate and follow outline of grassy path along lower slopes towards hill. Make for gate and cross lane to join bridleway. Keep **L** at fork, by bridleway waymark, and walk along to head of Uffington's **White Horse**.

❷ Descend steeply on path to tarmac access road, keeping chalk figure on your immediate **L**. If you prefer to avoid dramatic descent, retrace your steps to lane, turn **R** and continue to junction with **B4507**. Cross and take road towards **Uffington**, turning **L** at path ('Woolstone'). Cross stile and keep hedge on **R**. Make for 2 stiles in field corner. Continue across next field to stile and cut through trees to next stile. Keep ahead with hedgerow on your **L**.

❸ Cross stile, turn **L** at road and walk through **Woolstone**. Turn **L** by White Horse Inn and follow road to **All Saints Church**. As you approach it, veer **R** across churchyard to stile and gate. Cross paddock to

further gate and stile. Turn **L** up road. Turn **R** at footpath sign. Follow edge of field, keeping hedge on your L-H side, eventually reaching stile. Turn **R** and walk through trees to footbridge. Cross footbridge to field, head diagonally **L** to stile; turn **R**. Follow field edge to stile within sight of thatched **cottage**. Cross it and continue to another stile leading out to road. Cottage is now level with you on **L**.

❹ Cross road; follow D'Arcy Dalton Way, signposted on opposite side. Make for stile, cross paddock and head for road by sign ('Compton Beauchamp'). Cross and take drive to **church**, next to **manor**. Retrace your steps to sign and walk up to meet junction with B4507. Cross and climb quite steeply to **Ridgeway**.

❺ Turn **R** to visit **Wayland's Smithy** or **L** to continue. Follow track to crossroads ('Woolstone') and continue on **Ridgeway** uphill to reach ramparts of **Uffington Castle** on **L**. Leave track here, cut through remains of fort to access road and return to car park.

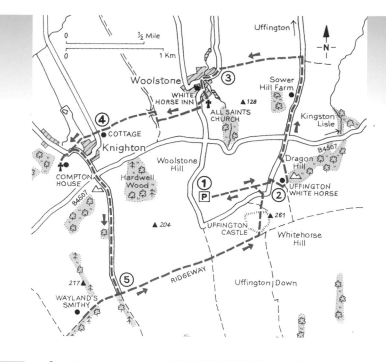

Stonor Religious Refuge

3½ miles (5.7km) 1hr 15min **Ascent:** 150ft (46m)

Paths: Wood and parkland paths and tracks, country lanes, 2 stiles
Suggested map: OS Explorer 171 Chiltern Hills West
Grid reference: SU 735883
Parking: Off-road at southern end of Stonor, by barns of Upper Assendon Farm, which straddle road

Across a beautiful deer park.

❶ The chief attraction is **Stonor Park** and the Elizabethan house. **Stonor** has a 14th-century Chapel of the Holy Trinity. During the 16th and 17th centuries it was used as refuge for Catholics and the family endured persecution and imprisonment as a result of their devotion to the faith. Make for 30mph speed restriction sign at southern end of **Stonor**. Turn **L** at stile just beyond it to join footpath. Keep farm outbuildings on **L** and go up slope towards trees. Cross stile into woodland and begin climbing very steeply into Chilterns. Look for white arrows on tree trunks and further up reach clear track on bend. Keep ahead, cross track and pass beside **Coxlease Farm**.

❷ Keep to **R** of outbuildings and join track leading to farmhouse. Make for road; turn **L**. Pass several houses and follow lane between hedges. Avoid path on **R** and, further on, road bends sharp **R**. Ignore bridleway on **L** for **Stonor** and keep on road, which

curves **L** and runs alongside **Kildridge Wood**. Pass some double wooden gates on **R** and keep to road as it curves **R**. Turn **L** after a few paces, signposted towards Southend.

❸ Keep Kildridge Wood on **L** still, with views over fields and rolling countryside on **R**. Follow lane until you reach turning on **L** – the **Chiltern Way**. Follow path beside pair of brick-and-flint cottages, following the way towards **Stonor Park**. Cross junction of tracks and descend between trees. Some of the trunks carry CW symbol for **Chiltern Way**. Keep **L** at fork, passing between laurel bushes and trees, and eventually you reach deer fence and gate.

❹ Pass alongside tall wire fence and gradually view of Stonor house edges into view. Head down towards road and look for kissing gate in deer fence. Turn **L** and head for **Stonor Arms**. Pass footpath and turning to Maidensgrove and keep ahead to **Stonor Arms**. Continue through village and return to parking area.

Dorchester A Very Special Abbey

4½ miles (7.2km) 1hr 45min **Ascent:** 115ft (35m) ⚠

Paths: Field and woodland paths and tracks, stretch of Thames Path and main road with pavement

Suggested map: OS Explorer 170 Abingdon, Wantage

Grid reference: SU 578939

Parking: Parking area in Bridge End at southern end of Dorchester

An ancient settlement with superb views.

❶ From parking area walk towards centre of **Dorchester**, keeping **abbey church** on R. As you approach **Fleur de Lys**, turn **L** into Rotten Row and walk to Mayflower Cottage and Pilgrims. Take path between the 2 properties and pass beside allotments. At row of cottages, veer **L** to follow track. Swing **R** after 60yds (55m) at sign for Day's Lock. Pass between fencing and out across large field. Ahead is outline of **Wittenham Clumps**. At low embankment of **Dyke Hills**, turn **R** in front of fence.

❷ Follow path along field edge, pass over track and continue. Path, enclosed by hedge and fencing, heads south towards **Thames** river bank. Go through gate and follow path, now unfenced, to footbridge at **Day's Lock**. Cross river to Lock House Island and head for **St Peter's Church** at Little Wittenham.

❸ Turn **L** just beyond it, at entrance to manor. Keep **R** at immediate fork, go through gate and begin steep climb to viewpoint on **Round Hill** at top. Veer **L** as you approach seat, pass 2nd seat and keep **L** at next fork, heading for **Castle Hill**. Head towards gates at foot of hill, avoid stile and go through gate, up flight of steps and into trees. At T-junction, turn **L**.

❹ Emerge from trees and pass commemorative stone, keeping it on R. Descend grassy slope to gate and pass through trees to field. Continue along perimeter, with woodland L. Pass stile, continue along field edge and round to R in corner. Swing **L** to join nature trail; follow it through **Little Wittenham Wood**.

❺ At a barrier and T-junction in heart of wood, turn **L** and follow path back to Little Wittenham. Recross Thames then turn **R** to follow river downstream. On reaching confluence of Thames and **Thame**, swing **L** and head north towards Dorchester. As Thame bends R, keep ahead to gate. Keep to **R** of Dyke Hills to another gate and skirt field to track (Wittenham Lane). Pass Catholic Church of St Birinus to reach car park.

Wightwick Along the Canal

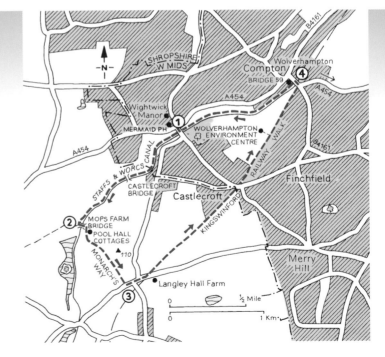

4½ miles (7.2km) 1hr 30min **Ascent:** 59ft (18m) ⚠

Paths: Canal tow path, disused railway track and field paths, 1 stile

Suggested map: OS Explorer 219 Wolverhampton & Dudley

Grid reference: SP 870982

Parking: Near Mermaid pub, Wightwick

An easy family walk.

❶ From car park, cross A454 at pedestrian crossing to enter Windmill Lane. Bear **R** and descend to tow path of **Staffordshire and Worcestershire Canal**, heading in southwesterly direction. Initially tow path leads along back of private residences. After passing Cee-Ders Club (on far side of canal), you reach open countryside, with ducks, coots and moorhens for company. This stretch of the canal is similar to a river and you are likely to see anglers fishing for perch, roach, chub, bream or carp. You may even see a colourful narrowboat pass by. Continue beneath bridge No 55 (**Castlecroft Bridge**) and along tow path until you come to bridge No 54 (**Mops Farm Bridge**).

❷ Leave tow path and cross bridge. Go **R** past Pool Hall Cottages and follow waymarkers of **Monarch's Way**, heading generally southeast. At first, path is to R of field hedge then, later, it crosses over to L-H side until you come to stile to reach Langley Road.

❸ Go **L** along road to junction and then bear **R** through small gateway to descend to dismantled railway. Head **L** and follow **Kingswinford (South Staffordshire) Railway Walk**. This is easy walking and you are likely to meet a number of other walkers and possibly cyclists. Continue for about 2 miles (3.2km). You will eventually pass beneath road bridge near **Castlecroft**; following this there are moments when the scene opens up to give lovely views. After passing **Wolverhampton Environment Centre** you come to **Compton**. Leave disused railway line and climb up to **A454**, going **L**.

❹ Go **L** again and descend by side of **Bridge No 59** restaurant on to tow path and take it back to bridge No 56, passing couple of lock gates and number of moored narrowboats. Go beneath Bridge No 56 and leave canal on to pavement of Windmill Lane. Continue towards main **A454** road and cross over to return to **Mermaid** pub in **Wightwick**.

Sandwell Valley Mines and Monasteries

4 miles (6.4km) 1hr 30min **Ascent:** 66ft (20m) ⚠
Paths: Lakeside paths and tracks, no stiles
Suggested map: OS Explorer 220 Birmingham
Grid reference: SP 035927
Parking: RSPB visitor centre

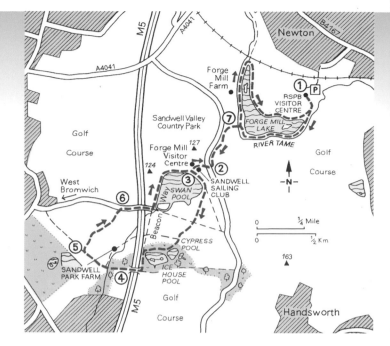

An RSPB nature reserve and country park reveals a spiritual and industrial legacy.

❶ Leave RSPB car park by going **L** of **visitor centre** building on to footpath. This leads down to strip of land between **River Tame** and **Forge Mill Lake**. Continue along footpath, which arcs gently **R**. As you work your way around lake you reach gateway where you go **L** over bridge across River Tame and continue on tarmac path/cycleway that leads down to Forge Lane.

❷ Cross busy lane with great care and walk to **R** of **Sandwell Sailing Club** premises, then bear **L** until you come to **Swan Pool**.

❸ Head **L** and stroll around side of pool for 150yds (137m), then bear **L** again on to footpath that leads across meadowland away from water's edge. Soon you enter hedged footpath heading generally southwest. At junction of paths go **L** and proceed through trees, then go **R** to follow path to north of **Cypress** and **Ice House** pools. You will emerge on to

tarmac lane by side of noisy M5. (If you had continued ahead at junction of paths instead of going **L** you would have arrived at same position.) Go **L** and stroll along this wide lane. At junction, bear **R** and take footbridge over M5.

❹ Follow tarmac path up to **Sandwell Park Farm** where there are toilets and you can get refreshments.

❺ Go **R** opposite to farm buildings and walk along signed public footpath heading northeastwards into trees. (To **L** you will see golf practice area.) When you reach end of hedged area bear **L** and proceed along tarmac path until you reach junction.

❻ Go **R** here along Salters Lane and return over M5 via 2nd footbridge. Take tarmac path that goes to **L** of **Swan Pool** and continue past **sailing club** premises to busy Forge Lane. Cross lane and take footbridge back over **River Tame** to reach junction of footpaths by edge of **Forge Mill Lake**.

❼ Go **L**; walk around lake back to **visitor centre**.

Walsall Woodland and the Waterfront

3¾ miles (6km) 1hr 15min **Ascent:** 66ft (20m) ⚠
Paths: Field paths and tow paths, 2 stiles
Suggested map: OS Explorer 220 Birmingham
Grid reference: SK 041910
Parking: Hay Head Wood Nature Reserve car park

Along the canal tow paths to Park Lime Pits.

❶ From car park proceed over **Longwood Lane** through parking area on to **Longwood Bridge** and descend to tow path of **Rushall Canal**. Go **L** (southwest) and walk along side of very straight part of canal.

❷ After 650yds (594m) you reach bridge, which crosses over canal where you go off to **R** and join footpath that leads around bottom end of **golf course**. Follow blue-topped white posts and continue past rear of gardens, with golf course to your **R**, and along back of **playing fields**. After passing exit area to B4151, continue ahead on tarmac driveway that leads to municipal golf course's main car park and large recreational area. Leave car park at its rear and continue along tarmac path by **L** side of stream. After about 700yds (640m), turn **R**, over stone footbridge, and walk to **R-H** side of play area up to tarmac driveway.

❸ Head **R**, up driveway to leave park area, then cross over Buchannan Road and continue up footpath until you reach Argyle Road. Go **R** along Argyle Road which arcs **L**, and look out for footpath sign. Go **R** and take hedged/fenced footpath along back of houses in Fernleigh Road. This emerges on to **A454** (Aldridge Road).

❹ Cross over **A454** and go **R** along its grass verge for 220yds (201m), then go **L** over stile by footpath sign ('Riddian Bridge'). Continue along footpath following series of fingerposts until you come to **Riddian Bridge** on **Wyrley and Essington Canal**.

❺ Descend to tow path (part of the **Beacon Way**) turn **R** and walk along it. This is easy walking, with just a few ducks and perhaps a heron or two for company and you may see fishermen on the banks of the canal. In about ½ mile (800m) you come to **Longwood Bridge**. Exit here on to A454. Cross canal and bear **R** to return to car park.

69 Sutton Park A Wild Experience

7¼ miles (11.7km) 2hrs 30min **Ascent:** 230ft (70m) ▲
Paths: Footpaths, tracks and road in parkland
Suggested map: OS Explorer 220 Birmingham
Grid reference: SP 112961
Parking: Visitor centre car park, Sutton Park

A longer walk visiting the largest National Nature Reserve in the West Midlands.

❶ Walk from car park to entrance road and go **L** up to **Keeper's Pool**. At bottom of pool, bear **R** through gate and follow edge of pool, then go northwards through trees on path until you reach **Blackroot Pool**. Walk along **L** edge of pool for about 220yds (201m), then bear **L** (northwest) and take track through woodland of **Upper Nut Hurst**. In about ½ mile (800m), turn **R** and then cross railway track to arrive at **Bracebridge Pool**.

❷ Turn **R**, along edge of pool, and at end bear **R** along track. Go through car park and then **L** along park road for about 100yds (91m) on to track leading into woodland of **Gum Slade**. Continue to junction of paths, then go **L** across grassy clearing. Proceed into woodland on track that arcs **L** and gently descends to cross footbridge at end of Bracebridge Pool.

❸ Follow track as it arcs **L** and then **R** to cross railway line again. Continue along track until you reach road, then go **R** for 750yds (686m) up to wide straight track.

❹ Head **L** and walk along this track for 1 mile (1.6km). Cross small brook and walk beside **golf course** to road exit from park. Don't leave park; instead cross road and bear **L** along pathway through trees of **Westwood Coppice** until you come to car park by **Banners Gate**.

❺ Bear **L** up road, passing to **R** of **Longmoor Pool**. About 90yds (82m) beyond end of pool, head **R** along track. After passing to **R** of trees, cross open grass area close to **Powell's Pool** to reach roadway near **Boldmere Gate**.

❻ Go **L** along road for 130yds (121m), then **R**, through edge of Wyndley Wood. In 220yds (201m) bear **R** on to straight road that leads to cattle grid and ford at end of **Wyndley Pool**. Continue ahead to return to **visitor centre**.

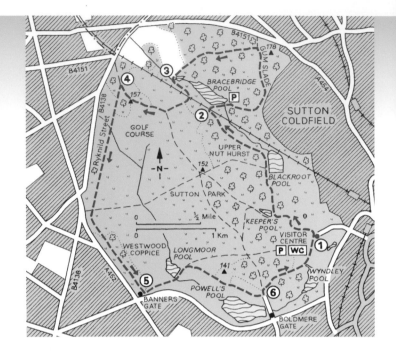

70 Berkswell An Ancient Parish

4½ miles (7.2km) 1hr 30min **Ascent:** 115ft (35m) ▲
Paths: Field paths and parkland footpaths, 13 stiles
Suggested map: OS Explorer 221 Coventry & Warwick
Grid reference: SP 244791
Parking: Free car park near church in Berkswell

A walk around Berkswell, an ancient Saxon town with an intriguing five-holed stocks and two historic pubs.

❶ From car park, near **church** in Berkswell, follow **Heart of England Way** to Meriden Road. Go **L** along this road for 300yds (274m), then cross over and go **R** up farm lane, passing **Blind Hall Farm**.

❷ At end of lane/track cross stile by farm gate, bear **L** and walk along field edge to its **L** corner. Go **L** over 2 stiles and continue ahead by hedge. Waymarked footpath weaves in and out of hedge. After going through wide hedge gap, walk to field corner and go **L** past small pond until you come to some houses in **Four Oaks**. Bear **L**, cross over large cultivated field diagonally and exit on to Meriden Road. Cross road and continue down driveway to **R** of **Wilmot Cottage** opposite, going through gateway onto farmland. Path goes to **R** of hedge, offering clear view of Home Farm to **L**, then crosses field diagonally. In about 625yds (571m) you will reach corner of Mercote Hall Lane.

❸ Go **L** along lane for about ½ mile (800m), passing Park Farm complex. Walk along lane past large enclosed **sand and gravel pits**.

❹ At end of pit area go **L** along footpath and over footbridges, ascending to **L** of hedge on approach to **Marsh Farm**.

❺ Just beyond farm, turn **L** and follow farm track towards **Sixteen Acre Wood**. Cross stile into wood and take track along wood edge for some 700yds (640m). Continue by hedge and go through strip of trees into parkland. Follow path for some 650yds (594m) and then enjoy a magnificent view of **Berkswell Hall Lake** before entering trees and going through kissing gate to rejoin **Heart of England Way**. Cross track and stile on to planked area with **Berkswell Hall** to your **L**. Continue through gates back into Berkswell. Just after going through church gate, bear **L** to return to car park.

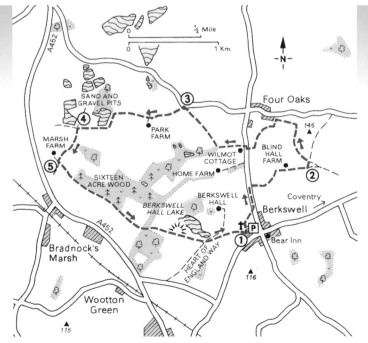

Bedworth The Canals

4½ miles (7.2km) 1hr 30min **Ascent:** 56ft (17m)
Paths: Lanes, field paths, woodland tracks and tow paths, 3 stiles
Suggested map: OS Explorer 221 Coventry & Warwick
Grid reference: SP 364839
Parking: Near Elephant and Castle in Hawkesbury

An easy walk to see Hawkesbury Junction where the Coventry and Oxford canals meet.
❶ From **Elephant and Castle** pub ascend to Coventry Road. Go **L**, crossing bridge over **Oxford Canal**, and follow road past **Old Crown** pub.
❷ In about 250yds (229m), just before large sign for Bedworth and Nuneaton, go **R** and take footpath into meadowland. Continue along footpath to stile and then go **L** over stile into large field. Cross over field, heading towards double stile at end, but don't go over it.
❸ Go **L** again and head towards another stile in field corner. Cross this and continue in northeasterly direction. Your route passes by **Trossachs Farm** (on L) and you continue along path by field edge. After going over footbridge, walk diagonally over large hay field, aiming to **L** of oak tree in far corner.
❹ Cross stile near this tree, then **L** to join **Coventry Way**. Take footpath by field edge over several fields until you exit on to Coventry road once again, near to

Mile Tree Farm. Cross road and continue ahead on footpath heading generally towards **Hollyhurst Farm**. Path arcs **L** and you go through hedge gap into area being prepared as nature reserve – this is called **Coalpit Fields Woodlands**. Keep to **L** and go over stile on to farm track. Follow this track as it arcs **L** to reach bridge over **Coventry Canal**.
❺ Just before reaching bridge, go **L** and descend to tow path along this pleasant stretch of canal. Head south along tow path – this is part of **Centenary Way**. Path arcs gently **R** (southwest) and soon you reach **Hawkesbury Junction**. The junction was also known as Sutton Stop, after the name of the first lock keeper, and it became a famous resting place for bargees on this part of the canal system. Today you'll see lots of narrowboats and find the **Greyhound** pub.
❻ Leave Coventry Canal and go **L** along **Oxford Canal** tow path. Walk beneath electricity pylons and make your way back to **Elephant and Castle** pub.

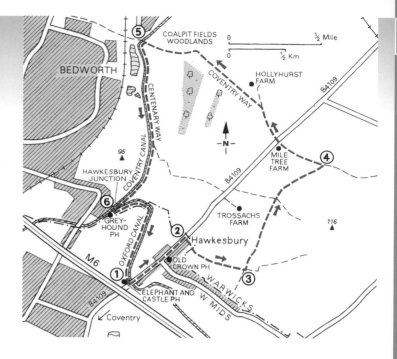

Edge Hill Theatre of War

3½ miles (5.7km) 1hr 30min **Ascent:** 280ft (85m)
Paths: Field and woodland paths, country road, 6 stiles
Suggested map: OS Explorer 206 Edge Hill & Fenny Compton
Grid reference: SP 370481
Parking: Radway village

Climb a wooded escarpment and enjoy fine views over a Civil War battleground.
❶ Walk through **Radway** to church. Veer **L** into West End and pass alongside grounds of **The Grange** on your **L**. Curve **L** by pond and thatched cottages. **Methodist chapel** can be seen here. Follow lane as it becomes stony track and go through kissing gate into field. Walk ahead to stile and continue ahead across sloping field towards Radway Tower, now **Castle Inn**. Look for gap in hedge by inspection cover and maintain direction, climbing steeply towards wooded escarpment.
❷ Make for stile and enter wood. Continue straight over junction and follow markers for Macmillan Way up slope to road. With Castle Inn on your **R**, turn **L** for several paces to **R-H** path running between Cavalier Cottage and Rupert House. Make for stile, turn **L** at road and walk along to **Ratley**. When road bends **L** by copper beech tree, turn **R** to fork. Veer **R** and follow

High Street down and round to **L**. Pass **church** and keep **L** at triangular junction.
❸ With **Rose and Crown** to **R**, follow Chapel Lane and, when it bends **L**, keep ahead up steps to stile. Keep fence on **L** initially before striking out across field to stone stile in boundary hedge. Turn **R** and follow **Centenary Way** across field to line of trees. Swing **L** and now skirt field to gap in corner. Follow path down to galvanised kissing gate, cut across field to footbridge then head up slope to gap in field boundary.
❹ Turn **L** and follow road past bungalows. Pass **Battle Lodge** and make for junction. Cross over and join woodland path running along top of escarpment. On reaching steps on **L**, turn **R** and descend steeply via staircase known as **Jacobs Ladder**. Drop down to gate then follow path straight down field to a stile at bottom. Go through kissing gate beyond it then pass alongside private garden to reach drive. Follow it to road and turn **L** for centre of **Radway**.

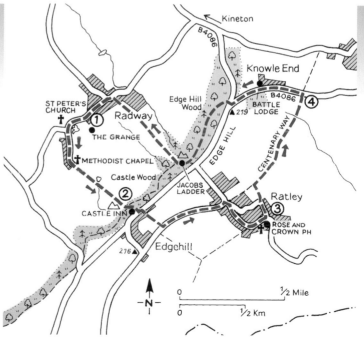

73 Studley A Priory Appointment

4¾ miles (7.7km) 1hr 15min **Ascent:** 49ft (15m) ▲
Paths: Field paths and parkland, 9 stiles
Suggested map: OS Explorer 220 Birmingham
Grid reference: SP 072637
Parking: Atcheson Close car park, Studley

A walk past a former castle and the site of a 12th-century priory.

❶ Walk down Needle Close to Alcester road; go **L** to traffic island. Cross and go to Priory Court on footpath to **L** of houses. Cross footbridge; bear **R** to stile into field, aiming towards 2nd stile at corner of field opposite. Head **L**; follow waymarker, going **L** alongside field hedge for about ½ mile (800m). Turn **R** at **The Dairy** and continue in northeasterly direction.

❷ Go **R** between buildings of **Field Farm** and walk along farm drive. In 100yds (91m), go **R** over stile crossing corner of field on to Hardwick Lane. Cross lane, walk between **Spinney Cottages**, then over parkland until you reach driveway near glasshouses. Cross over driveway, go through handgate and walk to **R** of cottage to enter wood. Follow footpath through trees and continue ahead by field edge until you reach end of woodland. Turn **L** and walk up farm track past duck pond and farm building.

❸ Go **R** to corner and cross next field diagonally to

footbridge, then ascend to **L** of **Morton Common Farm**. Follow farm drive to road. Go **R** along road for 150yds (137m), then **R** again over footbridge and cross over cultivated field. At farm gate, bear **R** and walk by field hedge on to farm track.

❹ Continue **R** along track. In about ½ mile (800m), it arcs **R**; turn **L** here across middle of field towards Studley's **Church of the Nativity of the Blessed Virgin Mary**. Go through overflow graveyard and enter main churchyard, passing church and leaving via lychgate on to lane.

❺ Go **L** and cross lane and stile. Descend through pastureland, cross footbridge over **River Arrow**, then bear **R** and walk along river bank towards **Studley**. A handgate leads into end of Wickham Road. Head **L** along side of housing estate; bear **R** into Gunners Lane. Go **L** up Castle Road to Alcester road, cross and ascend Needle Close to car park.

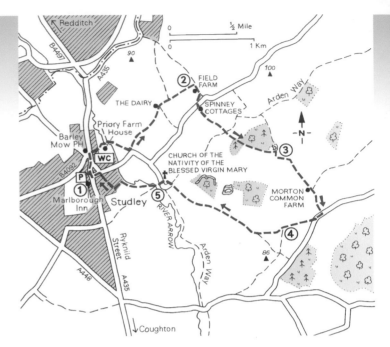

74 Alcester A Roman Town

5 miles (8km) 1hr 30min **Ascent:** 269ft (82m) ▲
Paths: Road pavements, field paths, woodland tracks and farm lanes, 6 stiles
Suggested map: OS Explorer 205 Stratford-upon-Avon & Evesham
Grid reference: SP 088573
Parking: Bleachfield car park, Alcester

An easy walk through an old Roman town, woodland and attractive villages.

❶ From car park enter Bleachfield Street and go **L** to old Stratford Road. Cross over road and wander up High Street. Bear **R** past impressive St Nicholas Church and, at corner of road, turn **R** down Malt Mill Lane. At bottom of lane, go **L** through public gardens and follow tarmac footpath by side of River Arrow to reach old Stratford Road again. Cross road and go down lane opposite into Oversley Green village, passing by Alcester football club's ground, then crossing bridge over **River Arrow**.

❷ At road junction bear **L** and in 80yds (73m) go **R** along hedged footpath behind row of houses and past golf driving range. Soon you will bear **R** and then **L** to reach junction of paths. Go **R** here across pastureland close to **Oversley Hill Farm** before coming to Severn Trent sub station.

❸ Go **R**, under **A46** road bridge, and bear **R** through

gateway into **Oversley Wood**. Take stone track into wood for about 400yds (366m) and then go **L**. In further 400yds (366m) track arcs **R** and continues westwards, descending back to main track. Now go **L** for 650yds (594m), then **R** to leave wood over stile.

❹ Go **R** and walk along edge of Oversley Wood to its corner. Continue ahead along hedged track until you reach farm lane, with **Oversley Castle** on hillock to **L**.

❺ Go **R** along lane and join **Heart of England Way**. Walk up lane towards some large grain silos by side of **Lower Oversley Lodge Farm**. From farm complex go down to footbridge, which crosses over busy A46. Cross and walk down Primrose Lane, passing beautiful thatched house. At T-junction go **L** along Mill Lane for about 650yds (594m).

❻ Just before reaching mobile home site, go **R**, down path and cross over footbridge over **River Arrow**. Path becomes lane by houses, with allotments to R. Walk up Bleachfield Street back to car park.

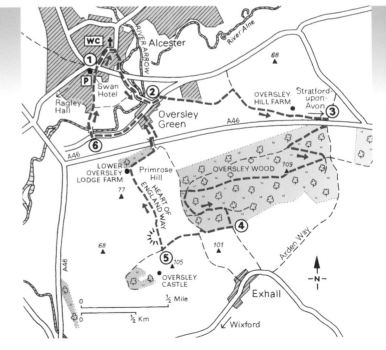

Henley-in-Arden Stratford-upon-Avon Canal

5 miles (8km) 2hrs **Ascent:** 180ft (55m)

Paths: Field paths, farm tracks and tow path, 11 stiles
Suggested map: OS Explorer 220 Birmingham
Grid reference: SP 152658
Parking: Prince Harry Road car park, Henley-in-Arden

A gentle walk around picturesque Henley-in-Arden, The Mount and the Stratford-upon-Avon Canal.

❶ After leaving car park at rear, walk through gardens until you come to Beaudesert Lane, opposite Beaudesert Church. Go **R** through kissing gate by church wall and follow waymarkers of **Heart of England Way** for steep but short ascent to top of **The Mount**. Enjoy the fine views over Henley-in-Arden. Continue over old earthworks of the former **castle** of the de Montfort family until you reach corner of top far field. Go over stile and continue along footpath, which runs to **L** of hedge.

❷ In about 220yds (201m), leave Heart of England Way by going **R** and diagonally crossing next field to come to lane in **Kite Green**. Go **L** along lane for about ¼ mile (400m) and then turn **R** over stile on to footpath, which arcs gently to **R**. In middle of next field bear **L** and proceed in easterly direction towards Church Farm.

❸ Go through gate to **R** of farm buildings on to lane. Turn **R** and follow lane, passing by **Manor Farm** to reach A4189 Henley to Warwick road. Go **L** along road for about 220yds (201m), then cross it.

❹ Immediately after passing canal bridge, descend on to tow path of **Stratford-upon-Avon Canal** via gate and take this back towards **Henley-in-Arden**. Cross canal bridge and tarmac track/lane opposite. In 180yds (165m), this bends sharp **L**, bringing you to road near Pettiford Bridge. Turn **R** over bridge.

❺ In 50yds (46m), go **L** into pastureland. Path arcs **R**, diagonally over field. Cross stile in far **L** corner to reach banks of **River Alne**. Take riverside path then, at junction, bear **R** and proceed ahead, passing to **R** of **Blackford Mill Farm** buildings. Continue on field paths to **L** of **Blackford Hill** to reach **A4189** road in **Henley-in-Arden**. Cross road going **L**, then **R** on to Prince Harry Road which leads back to car park.

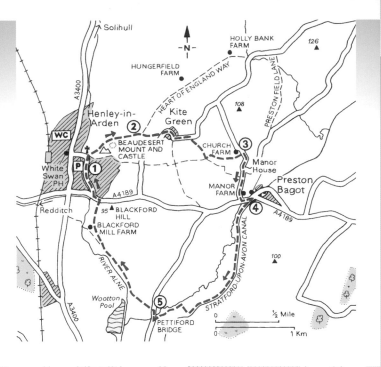

Kingsbury A Water Park

3 miles (4.8km) 1hr **Ascent:** 33ft (10m)

Paths: Reservoir paths and footpaths, 1 stile
Suggested map: OS Explorer 232 Nuneaton & Tamworth
Grid reference: SP 217962
Parking: Pear Tree Avenue car park (free)

A lovely stroll through old Kingsbury and around the pools of its water park.

❶ From car park, go **L** along Pear Tree Avenue to reach A51. Go **R** along pavement then cross road passing in front of **White Swan** pub. About 20yds (18m) just before pub, cross road and go **L** along footpath by side of churchyard. Follow **Heart of England** waymarkers past church and descend steps to reach footbridge over **River Tame**. Cross bridge and walk along raised footway planks to enter **Kingsbury Water Park**. The water park was once 620 acres (251ha) of old sand and gravel pits, but it has been developed into a major leisure facility with more than 30 lakes attracting 200,000 visitors each year. With **Hemlingford Water** close on your **L**, walk by side of **Bodymoor Heath Water**, leaving **Heart of England** behind keep ahead to reach **visitor centre**.

❷ From visitor centre follow signs to sailing club along lanes and footpaths. As you veer to **L**, walk by side of **Bodymoor Heath Water** then pass by entrance gate to **Tamworth Sailing Club**. Continue to R-H side of **Bodymoor Heath Water**, along mixture of tarmac lane and grass footpaths.

❸ At end of stretch of water bear **L**, then **R** and follow waymarkers for **Centenary Way**. These take you near Swann Pool and then between **Mill Pool** and **Hemlingford Water** as your route veers northeast. Shortly you will reach gateway and then cross over **Hemlingford Bridge**.

❹ Walk along tarmac lane towards busy A51, but just before reaching it go **L** over stile and cross edge of field to final stile on to pavement of **A51**, near middle of **Kingsbury**. Go **L** along pavement until you reach area of open land on other side of road. Cross over road and go **R**, through kissing gate on to clear footpath that goes along back of some houses. In about 220yds (201m), turn **L** into Meadow Close, then **L** again into Pear Tree Avenue to return to car park.

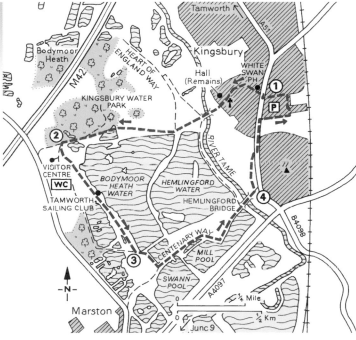

77 Baddesley Clinton A Medieval Manor House

5 miles (8km) 2hrs **Ascent:** 16ft (5m) ⚠
Paths: Field paths and woodland tracks, 3 stiles
Suggested map: OS Explorer 221 Coventry & Warwick
Grid reference: SP 204713
Parking: Lane near church at Baddesley Clinton Manor

A fine church, woodland and the opportunity to visit a superb National Trust property.

❶ Take the short detour to visit **Baddesley Clinton Manor** – a fine medieval moated manor house. From driveway to church, walk to Hay Wood Lane. Cross lane, turn **L**, then **R** and walk down track opposite, passing by **Old Keeper's Lodge** on way into **Hay Wood**. Follow track through wood to emerge via gate. Head for another gate to **L** of **Wood Corner Farm**. Go through yet another gate to arrive on farm drive. Go **L** along drive, passing close to farmhouse building. This soon brings you to **A4141**.

❷ Go **L** along grass verge of **A4141** for about 220yds (201m), then cross it and go **R** along bridlepath between buildings of **Abbey Farm**. Continue until you reach School Lane and walk **R** along it towards **A4141**. About 100yds (91m) before you reach end of lane, go **R** over stile and cross corner of field to reach **A4141** near Ducklings Day Nursery.

❸ Cross **A4141**, enter **Wroxall Abbey park** through pair of gates. Benedictine nuns founded the abbey in 1135 and it was purchased in 1710 by Sir Christopher Wren as his retreat. Follow track through grounds. In 500yds (457m) you go fairly close to old abbey building. Where track veers **L**, continue towards gate set to **L** of small area of enclosed woodland. Follow path as it goes to **R** of **Gilbert's Coppice** and continue in southwesterly direction to stile. Cross stile; take path to **L** of hedge to Quarry Lane.

❹ Go **R** along lane. Bear **L** at junction; keep along Rowington Green Lane for almost ½ mile (800m).

❺ Pass by former **windmill** on L and just before reaching **Lyons Farm**, go **R** through gate on to track which is part of **Heart of England Way**. Route takes you to **R** of farm complex along path/track going over stile and through several gates. After passing **Rowington Coppice** you come to handgate on to entrance driveway of the church and start.

78 Stratford-upon-Avon In the Bard's Footsteps

2½ miles (4km) 1hr **Ascent:** Negligible ⚠
Paths: Riverside paths and street pavements, no stiles
Suggested map: OS Explorer 205 Stratford-upon-Avon & Evesham
Grid reference: SP 205547
Parking: Recreation Ground pay-and-display car park

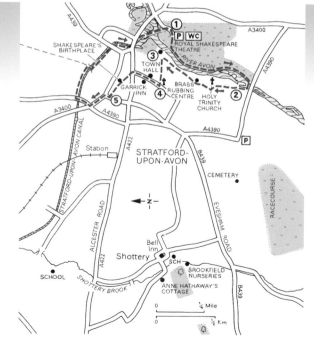

A tour of theatrical Stratford-upon-Avon to see the sights.

❶ From car park, walk along banks of River Avon opposite the famous **Royal Shakespeare Theatre**. Pass weir until you come to footbridge over river, just in front of A4390 road bridge.

❷ Go **R** over footbridge and bear **R** past old mill building on Mill Lane. Continue up Mill Lane and go through churchyard of **Holy Trinity Church**, walking around church to see river view. Leave churchyard through main gate into Old Town and follow pavement. Just before reaching turn into Southern Lane, go **R** into New Place Gardens and walk up to **Brass Rubbing Centre**. Continue past ferry and stroll through attractive Theatre Gardens by side of Avon, exiting into Waterside and passing by frontage of old theatre building.

❸ Go **L** up Chapel Lane, taking time to wander through Knot Gardens on your way up to Chapel

Street. At top of lane is Guild Chapel to Shakespeare's Grammar School, with New Place Gardens to your R.

❹ Go **R** along Chapel Street, passing Shakespeare Hotel and **Town Hall** into High Street. Harvard House is on L, near black-and-white **Garrick Inn**. At end of High Street, bear **L** around traffic island into Henley Street and walk along pedestrianised area that takes you past **Shakespeare's Birthplace** and the Museum. At top of Henley Street, bear **R** and then **L** into Birmingham Road. Cross road at pedestrian crossing and go **L** up to traffic lights.

❺ Head **R** up Clopton Road for 100yds (91m), then descend to tow path of **Stratford-upon-Avon Canal**. Follow this, going southeast. Cross over canal at bridge No 68 and continue along tow path into Bancroft Gardens by canal basin where you will see an array of colourful narrowboats and the Royal **Shakespeare Theatre**. Cross old Tram Bridge to car park on R.

Polesworth Monastic Lines

4 miles (6.4km) 1hr 30min **Ascent:** 115ft (35m) ▲

Paths: Canal tow paths, field paths and residential areas, 3 stiles

Suggested map: OS Explorer 232 Nuneaton & Tamworth

Grid reference: SK 262024

Parking: Hall Court car park (free)

Polesworth and its ancient abbey church.

❶ From car park at Hall Court, walk into Bridge Street and bear **L** towards bridge. After walking 25yds (23m), turn **L** into alleyway that leads to public footpath ('River Anker'). Cross footbridge over river, then bear **L** through gardens by riverside on footpath that arcs gently **R** towards bridge No 51 over **Coventry Canal**. Descend to canal; turn **L** along tow path, which you follow for 1½ miles (2.4km). Before walking beneath railway line look up to **R** and on far bank you will see **obelisk** on Hoo Hill. Stiper's Hill is to L. Continue beneath main electrified railway line.

❷ Leave Coventry Canal's tow path at bridge No 49 and ascend on to road going generally northwest past **Kitchens Bridge Cottage**. Soon after passing cottage look out for hedge gap on **L-H** side and proceed through this to cross footbridge over railway line. Now climb hill passing through farm gate close to buildings of **Dordon Hall** farm and continue up to road. Go **L**

along road; turn **R** at junction, following signpost to Dordon. Continue along Dunne Lane into village.

❸ Immediately after passing house, '**Lyndon Lea**', turn to **R** down track that leads to stile on to footpath over open farmland. Follow this footpath, heading generally northwards, towards prominent trees of **The Hollies**. Continue past trees, crossing couple of stiles and soon you will find yourself walking along stone track that becomes Common Lane on approach to **Polesworth**. Take pavement of lane through residential estate until you reach B5000 Tamworth to Grendon road. Cross road (take care, it can be busy) and stroll down to park area by **River Anker**; cross back over footbridge. Public footpath now leads up to junction of paths where you go **R**, towards **abbey**. Bear **L** and leave through Old Nunnery Gateway on to High Street. Now turn **L** and continue along High Street, past **Nethersole Centre** and turn **L** again into Bridge Street to return to Hall Court car park.

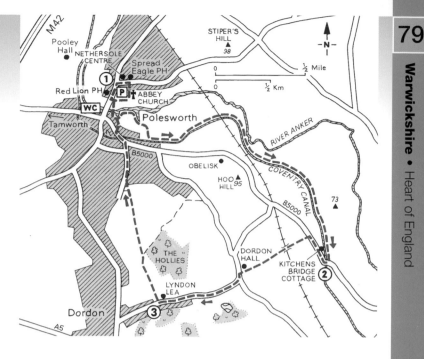

Charlecote Park An Elizabethan Jewel

5 miles (8km) 1hr 30min **Ascent:** 33ft (10m) ▲

Paths: Field paths and farm tracks, 2 stiles

Suggested map: OS Explorer 205 Stratford-upon-Avon

Grid reference: SP 262564

Parking: National Trust visitors car park for Charlecote Park

An easy walk into open countryside.

❶ From **Charlecote Park** car park, go **L** along grass verge and cross over **River Dene**. In about 100yds (91m), go **L** along wide track that arcs **L** on to clear fenced path by side of river and walk along for this 1½ miles (2.4km) into **Wellesbourne**. It was recorded in the Domesday Book as Walesborne. You will pass **weir** before you reach footbridge near St Peter's Church.

❷ Go **L** over footbridge and up fenced path to **L** of church until you reach village. Continue up road to **L** of house No 21 – **Kings Head** pub is on L. Cross main road in village and walk up Warwick Road opposite.

❸ In about 300yds (274m), just after passing Daniell Road, go **R** along tarmac path at back of houses. Cross footbridge and continue over several fields. Take footpath to **L** of copse of trees then go **R** into woodland. Turn **L** along track at top of hedge of trees. You will emerge from trees for short distance and then re-enter again. After you emerge for second time, look for hedge gap to **L**.

❹ Go through gap and then along footpaths to **Middle Hill Farm**.

❺ Continue **L**, between farm buildings then go to **R** of farmhouse and walk along farm drive for about ¾ mile (1.2km), passing entrance to **Coppington Farm** on way to **A429**. Cross road with care then stile opposite on to fenced footpath. After crossing minor road continue along driveway past farm building.

❻ In 100yds (91m), go **L** through kissing gate into pastureland. A 2nd kissing gate leads into large field that you walk around by field hedge. Go **R**, through further kissing gate, and continue to **R** of field hedge until you go through final kissing gate on to Charlecote Road. Go **L** along footway past thatched cottage into centre of **Charlecote**, then turn **R** along grass verge of main street past half-timbered houses and **Charlecote Pheasant Hotel**, with St Leonard's Church opposite, to reach **Charlecote Park** car park.

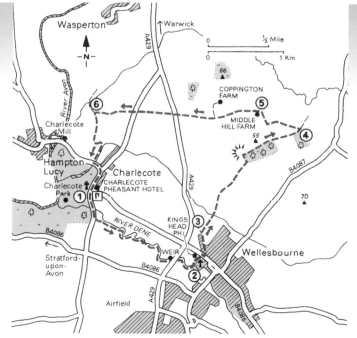

81 Warwick The Kingmaker Plot

5 miles (8km) 2hrs **Ascent:** 33ft (10m) ▲
Paths: Canal and riverside paths, street pavements, 2 stiles
Suggested map: OS Explorer 221 Coventry & Warwick
Grid reference: SP 277647
Parking: Racecourse car park

Along the canal to Warwick Castle.

❶ Walk to end of racecourse car park and go **L** towards golf **clubhouse**.

❷ Go **R** and take wide green track between golf course and driving range. In 300yds (274m), cross over racetrack and go over stile on to footpath by small factory. Continue ahead and, at corner of common land, go **R** over another stile on to lane and descend to road. Go **L** along pavement beneath railway bridge, then **L** again over stile on to grassland by Saltisford Canal. Follow grassy area to tow path, passing large narrowboat mooring area, and climb steps up to canal bridge on to pavement beside road. Go **R** along pavement and in 50yds (46m) you reach canal bridge over Grand Union Canal and busy A425.

❸ Cross road with care. Go **L** over canal bridge and descend to take tow path into **Warwick**, about 1½ miles (2.4km) away, passing by lock gate with **Cape of Good Hope** pub opposite and then going along back of houses. Shortly after passing by Tesco store and just before **aqueduct** over River Avon, go **L** down steps to join 'Waterside Walk'.

❹ Proceed **R** under aqueduct and follow river bank footpath. At **Castle Bridge**, climb steps on to pavement of A425 (Banbury) road; cross with care.

❺ Stroll on to bridge for views of the castle, then turn around and follow pavement towards Warwick.

❻ In 220yds (201m) go **L** and go down Mill Street for another view of castle. Return to main road and go **L** through main entrance gate to **Warwick Castle** grounds. Bear **R** and leave grounds via wall gate into Castle Street. Stroll up Castle Street passing by **Oken's House** until you reach tourist information centre on corner of High Street. St Mary's Church is ahead if you wish to visit. Turn **L** and walk along High Street, going under archway of **Lord Leycester's Hotel**. Go **R** into Bowling Green Street and, in 50yds (46m), turn **L** down Friars Street to reach racecourse.

82 Brailes Over the Hills

5 miles (8km) 1hr 30min **Ascent:** 476ft (145m) ▲
Paths: Field paths and country lanes, 7 stiles
Suggested map: OS Explorer 191 Banbury, Bicester & Chipping Norton
Grid reference: SP 308394
Parking: Village Hall car park in Lower Brailes – donation to hall funds expected

A fine hill walk with outstanding views.

❶ Leave car park by village hall in **Lower Brailes** to join B4035. Turn **L** to stroll up through village for ½ mile (800m), first passing post office then **George Hotel** (popular with local ramblers).

❷ Turn **R** and walk down waymarked public footpath by side of **George Hotel**. This runs beside small Cotswold dry-stone wall then crosses Cow Lane into pastureland. Continue ahead and, at junction of public footpaths, bear **L** to begin climb towards **New Barn Farm**. Footpath goes to **L** of farm and you should continue up hill, crossing several fields and stiles – there is a fine retrospective view over Lower Brailes. Walk up path, then go through hedge gap and bear **R**, walking above trees surrounding **Rectory Farm**.

❸ Bear **R** at end of trees and now begin gentle descent on farm track, enjoying view ahead over the valley as you proceed towards **Sutton-under-Brailes**. When you reach road at bottom of hill, turn **L** and wander through another beautiful Cotswold village, going to **R**, past fine village green, and heading for stile to **L-H** side of parish church.

❹ Clamber over stile and walk past church, then across field by **Church Farm** on to farm lane/track. Go **R** up this track, passing to **R-H** side of **Oaken Covert** as you ascend Cherington Hill.

❺ At junction of public footpaths, go **R** through metal bridle gate and follow tractor track heading generally eastwards. Route goes to **L-H** side of **New House Barn**, then veers roughly northeast along top of several farm fields, with more good views over Brailes Valley to **R**. After going through farm gate descend hedged track, High Lane, to Tommy's Turn.

❻ Turn **L** and walk down lane, continuing your descent into Henbrook Lane. Soon you will come back out on to High Street in **Lower Brailes** (B4035). Turn **R** along road for about 100yds (91m) to car park on corner of Castle Hill Lane.

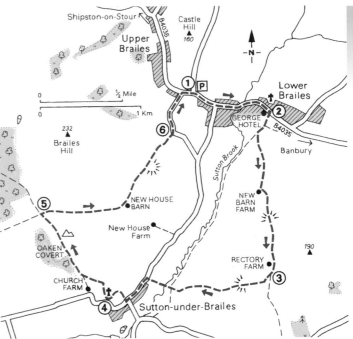

Hartshill Hayes Fine Views

4½ miles (7.2km) 1hr 30min **Ascent:** 295ft (90m) ⚠

Paths: Lanes, field paths, woodland tracks and tow paths, 3 stiles

Suggested map: OS Explorer 232 Nuneaton & Tamworth

Grid reference: SP 317943

Parking: Hartshill Hayes Country Park

A walk in a country park and along a canal.

❶ From car park enter **Hartshill Hayes Country Park** at back of visitor centre. Take path which arcs **L** (northwest) along top of Hartshill and enjoy view over the surrounding area. Continue ahead on path that descends gently into woodland. At bottom of woodland go over footbridge then bear **L** to walk along open path as you continue. In about ¼ mile (400m) path bends to **R** and you will ascend northeast to brow of hill from where you can overlook the **Coventry Canal**. Now path becomes hedged as you progress northwards towards **Quarry Farm**. Go through handgate to **L** of farm buildings on to Quarry Lane.

❷ Turn **R** and stroll down lane, bearing **R** at junction to reach bridge No 36 over Coventry Canal. Cross bridge and descend on to tow path, walking in northwesterly direction and under bridge No 37.

❸ Leave tow path at bridge No 38 and cross canal on to quiet lane. Walk up lane for 150yds (137m) then,

just before private house, go **L** through tall kissing gate into meadowland and on into pastureland. Cross over footbridge at bottom of field, then walk across next field and on to 2nd tall kissing gate and enter woodland of **Purley Park**. Follow footpath up **R** edge of woodland. Path arcs **L** into trees and you will exit on to Quarry Lane again.

❹ Go **R**; head up lane, past entrance to **Mancetter Quarry**. In further 600yds (549m), go **L** over stile.

❺ Walk to **R** of **Oldbury Farm** on good bridlepath going southeast. This path crosses pastureland, but soon you will be following white marker posts across **golf course**.

❻ Exit on to road then go **L**. Road passes by **Oldbury Grange** and Adbury Gardens. Where there is sharp R-H bend in road, go **L** up towards rear entrance to gardens and enter **Hartshill Hayes Country Park** via gate. Once you are in park bear **R** and join park path back to visitor centre.

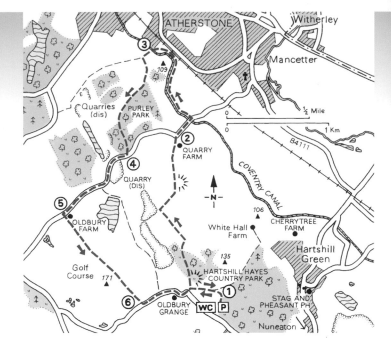

Dassett Into Fenny Compton

7¼ miles (11.7km) 2hrs 30min **Ascent:** 656ft (200m) ⚠

Paths: Field paths and farm tracks, 15 stiles Hilly countryside

Suggested map: OS Explorer 206 Edge Hill & Fenny Compton

Grid reference: SP 394523

Parking: Burton Dassett Hills Country Park car park – small charge

A walk in the Burton Dassett Hills.

❶ From car park in **country park** descend on footpath to **R** of **Bonfire Hill** into **Northend** to arrive at Hampden Court.

❷ Go **R** along main street for 300yds (274m), then **R** again through pair of kissing gates. Follow footpath heading generally eastwards towards Fenny Compton, crossing mixture of pastureland, fields and stiles.

❸ Enter **Fenny Compton** over stile, then head along Grant's Close into Avon Dassett road. Walk past Duckett Cottage and go through handgate to **R** of village church. Now bear **R** and cross over pastureland to road known as The Slade. Go **L** along road past large farm barn, then **R** over footbridge into large cultivated field. Follow footpath signs and cross this field to 2nd footbridge, then walk up next field, aiming for marker post in hedge ahead. Here go **L** and walk along field edge – from the top of the hill there is a fine view of the landmark four-sail windmill at Chesterton

and the Post Office Communication towers near Daventry. Follow direction of waymarkers, climb **Windmill Hill**, then descend over farm fields and hedged footpath into **Farnborough**, emerging on main street near **Butchers Arms** pub.

❹ Head **R**, along main street, and bear **R** past entrance gates to National Trust's **Farnborough Hall**. Continue up road to **L**, past lake, walking along footpath inside trees. At end of woodland continue along road for 500yds (457m) then go **R** over stile and cross 2 cultivated fields into pastureland. Descend to **L** of large barn, which brings you to **Avon Dassett**.

❺ Go **L** past church and in 75yds (69m) go **R** up track to **R** of **Avon Inn** into open countryside. Up to **R** is the impressive **Bitham Hall**. Waymarked footpath hugs top of fields until you arrive in **Burton Dassett**, passing by its lovely Norman church. Continue up road to return to car park near Beacon viewing point on **Magpie Hill** (630ft/192m).

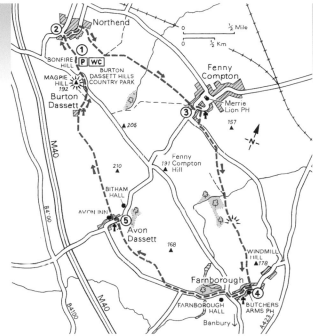

Draycote Water Two Historic Villages

6½ miles (10.4km) 2hrs **Ascent:** 164ft (50m) ⚠

Paths: Reservoir paths and field paths, 7 stiles

Suggested map: OS Explorer 222 Rugby & Daventry

Grid reference: SP 462690

Parking: Pay-and-display car park at Draycote Water

Around Warwickshire's largest reservoir and into Dunchurch and Thurlaston.

❶ From **Draycote Water** car park proceed up to reservoir then bear **R** following tarmac lane along top of **Farnborough Dam** wall to reach **Toft Bay**.

❷ At end of Toft Bay go **R** and leave reservoir grounds via handgate. Continue ahead then go **R** and follow waymarker signs to footpath that climbs past llama pens up towards **Toft House**. Continue along hedged footpath to **L** of house. This bends **L** on to lane where you go **R** up to **A426** Rugby to Dunchurch road. Go **L** along road, cross road bridge and enter **Dunchurch**, passing thatched houses. Village Square and St Peter's Church are R of crossroads, with **Dun Cow**, an old coaching inn, immediately opposite.

❸ At crossroads, go **L** along pavement of B4429 past the Dunchurch & Thurlaston WMC. Bear **L** along School Street and follow footpath past more thatched houses and infant **school** down to Dunchurch Scout

Group Hall. Here, go **R** then **L** along footpath to **R** of playing fields. Continue along hedged path and proceed to **R** of **Ryefield Farm**. Go ahead over pastureland then pass under M45 road bridge before diagonally crossing next field to 2 stiles to **Thurlaston**.

❹ Go to **L** by St Edmund's Church and down concrete farm track to handgate and footbridge to enter perimeter of **Draycote Water**.

❺ Go **R** along walkway by side of reservoir around **Biggin Bay**. To your R **Thurlaston Grange** can be seen, then you pass **golf course**. Continue around end of reservoir, passing by **treatment works**, and then stroll along **Draycote Bank**. To your R is spire of Bourton-on-Dunsmore church about 1 mile (1.6km) away; to its R is Bourton Hall. After passing by picnic area and just before reaching yachting area go **R** on footpath that leads up on to **Hensborough Hill** for a fine view. Meander past trig point, some 371ft (113m) above sea level, and return to car park.

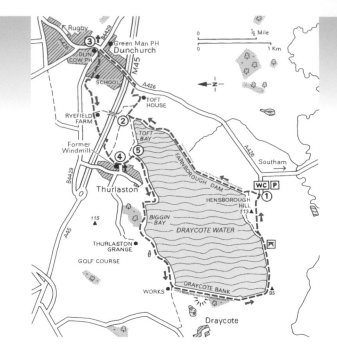

Longnor Peak Practice

6 miles (9.7km) 4hrs **Ascent:** 459ft (140m) ⚠

Paths: Some on road, otherwise good footpaths, can be muddy

Suggested map: OS Explorer OL24 White Peak

Grid reference: SK 089649

Parking: Longnor village square

The TV location of a popular medical drama.

❶ From square take road towards Buxton. Take 1st **R** into Church Street and go up lane, then **R**, up steps, to footpath. Follow waymarkers, behind some houses, over stile and along wall. Cross another stile, go downhill and turn **L** on to farm road.

❷ At fork go **L** then turn **R** on to road. After **Yewtree Grange** take farm road on **L**. At end of this road continue through gate on to footpath, through gap stile, downhill, across bridge and continue straight ahead. Eventually cross stile and turn **L** on to road.

❸ Fork **L** on to farm road, following waymarked path. Cross bridge by ford and follow path, by stream, to road. Turn **R** through **Hollinsclough**, following road to **R** and uphill. Turn **R** on to footpath, through gate and downhill.

❹ Fork **L** by 2 stones and continue along flank of hill. Cross stile then, at stone wall, fork **L** and uphill. At top turn **L** at stone gatepost, through **Moorside Farm**,

through kissing gate on to road. Turn **R** then cross stile to public footpath on **L**.

❺ Go downhill to stream and cross stile to **L** of ditch. Head uphill, under wire fence, through gap in wall and round field to gap stile. Turn back towards farm, then **L** on to well-signposted footpath to **Hill Top Farm**.

❻ Follow path over stiles and past farm to road. Cross it and take farm road to **L**. By small quarry, go **L** downhill, over stile and follow path along wall. Just before stream, cross stile on **L** and head uphill to **L** of some trees.

❼ Continue walking uphill, through gate in stone wall to some ruined buildings. Follow track to next farm, bear **L** after barn, then go **L** on to footpath uphill.

❽ Go through stile, follow wall uphill, over 2 stiles to road. Turn **L** then **R** towards **Longnor**. Just before road bends L, cross stile on **R**, go downhill and over several stiles to farm road. Turn **R** and follow this back to village.

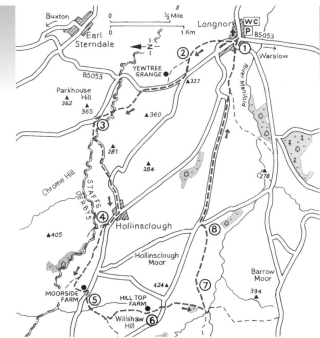

The Roaches Lud's Church

6¾ miles (10.9km) 4hrs **Ascent:** 1,020ft (311m)
Paths: Rocky moorland paths, forest tracks and road
Suggested map: OS Explorer OL24 White Peak
Grid reference: SK 006618
Parking: In lay-by opposite Windygates Farm; in summer park at Tittesworth Reservoir and catch bus

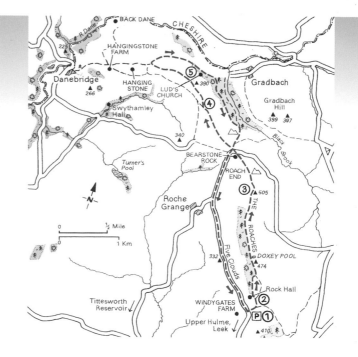

Follow in the footsteps of Sir Gawain, a Knight of the Round Table, and find the chapel of the Green Knight near the Roaches.

❶ From car park area go through gap stile and gate then continue uphill with wall on your R. At gate in wall turn L and cross over field. Go through another gate then uphill on rocky track. Go L through pair of stone gateposts and then continue R along this well-defined track.

❷ Path is flanked by rocks on R and woodland to L and below. Follow it to R and uphill through gap in rocks. Turn L and continue uphill. Continue following this ridge path. Pass to L of **Doxey Pool** and on towards trig point.

❸ From here descend on to paved path, past **Bearstone Rock** to join road at **Roach End**. Go through gap in wall, over stile and follow path uphill keeping wall on L. At signpost fork R on to concessionary path to **Danebridge**.

❹ Follow this path keeping straight ahead at crossroads, go over stile and up towards an outcrop. Carry on along ridge then head down to signpost by stile. Turn R and follow bridleway signed 'Gradbach'. At next signpost fork R towards Lud's Church. According to the 14th-century poem, *Sir Gawain and the Green Knight*, a knight on horseback gatecrashed a feast at Camelot and challenged the Knights of the Round Table. Sir Gawain rose to the challenge and beheaded the Green Knight. The latter retrieved his head and, laughing, he challenged Sir Gawain to meet with him again in a year's time at the Green Chapel – which has been identifield as **Lud's Chapel.**

❺ After exploring Lud's Church continue along path, through woodland, following signs for Roach End, eventually taking paved path uphill. Cross stile and continue walking with wall on your L-H side. When path reaches road, cross stile on to it and follow this road back to car park.

Tittesworth Reservoir Birds and Butterflies

4¼ miles (6.8km) 3hrs **Ascent:** 131ft (40m)
Paths: Good well-made footpaths, forest tracks and roads
Suggested map: OS Explorer OL24 White Peak
Grid reference: SK 999603
Parking: Near Middle Hulme Farm

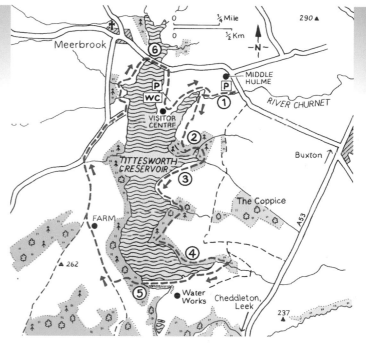

Reservoir biodiversity provides drinking water for the Potteries and a valuable wildlife habitat.

❶ Go through gate on to footpath and turn R. Cross 1st bridge, turn L then cross 2nd bridge and follow Long Trail/Short Trail direction signs along well-surfaced path. At junction beside picnic table turn L on to forest trail.

❷ Follow waymarked Long Trail through wood crossing bridge and some duckboarding then turn L at T-junction again following Long Trail. Follow path as it leaves wood and on to grassy area where it is less well defined but still visible.

❸ Continue along bank of **reservoir** then re-enter woodland, cross duckboards and continue once more on well-defined footpath. Cross bridge by picnic table, ascend steps and continue along duckboards. Skirt edge of wood, keeping fence on your L, then go downhill through wood and along reservoir bank.

❹ Go through some more woodland, cross bridge, walk up some steps then leave wood and continue on gravel path. Cross stile then follow path downhill towards dam. Go over stile and cross dam head. Cross stile at far end, go uphill on series of steps and turn R on to footpath.

❺ Cross stile and turn R at T-junction on to metalled lane. Continue ahead on this lane through **farm**, following signs for **Meerbrook**, straight ahead. At road junction cross over stile and turn R at Long Trail sign. Turn R again following road to **Tittesworth Reservoir**. When this turns to R, bear L on footpath beside reservoir.

❻ Cross stile on to road then turn R into public entrance to reservoir. Turn L at entrance to **visitor centre**, cross car park then go L at Nature Trail sign. Continue across grass then turn R on to concrete path. Follow this to 1st bridge and turn L to return to car park.

89 Cheddleton Flint Mill and Deep Hayes

3¼ miles (5.3km) 1hr 30min Ascent: 272ft (83m) ⚠

Paths: Tow path, tracks, grass paths and roads, 11 stiles

Suggested map: OS Explorer 258 Stoke-on-Trent

Grid reference: SJ 961533

Parking: Deep Hayes Country Park visitors' centre

Water, flint and the Staffordshire potteries.

❶ From visitors' centre in Deep Hayes Country Park go down to bottom of car park and cross stream before following shore of reservoir along wooded track. Path gains height above reservoir, but continues along shoreline. At fork of 2 obvious footpaths take L-H option down steep steps and across concrete stepping stones.

❷ Once across stream head R through stile with sign that says 'Keep dogs on leads'. After short while this track runs alongside small stream that fills pools of reservoir. When you cross back over stream, continue to follow stream to L through an aluminium kissing gate and along boardwalk.

❸ At junction of 3 paths (marked by signpost) head sharp L, back over stream for final time, before following footpath ('Cheddleton'). After crossing stile, go R for 30yds (27m) before heading up hill along wooded trail. At top of wood cross stile and go across

field, aiming for L of farm buildings, Shaffalong.

❹ In far corner of field, cross stile and go along muddy farm track to gate. After gate, continue ahead (rather than round to farm) to stile in wooden fence. Head diagonally R to stile, and again to another. From here go immediately L, keeping hedge to your L, before crossing stile.

❺ At obvious wooden public footpath sign, head across field following line of trees to your L. Cross small stile over dry-s7tone wall and cross to far side of next field. Just to L of clump of trees is stile followed in quick succession by another stile and slot in wall, bringing you out on to road into Cheddleton.

❻ At end of road, head L, with care, along A520 and, after 150yds (137m), turn L following signposts to flint mill. After exploring mill museum, keep going along canal tow path for 1 mile (1.6km) to bridge over canal. Cross bridge, before turning R, along driveway, to return to visitors' centre.

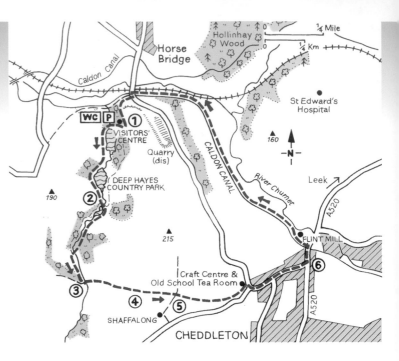

90 Grindon In the Lair of the White Worm

5 miles (8km) 2hrs 30 min Ascent: 423ft (129m) 🔺

Paths: Forest tracks, grass and mud, hard footpath

Suggested map: OS Explorer OL24 White Peak

Grid reference: SK 085545

Parking: At Grindon church

A limestone trail to the film location of Bram Stoker's last nightmare.

❶ From car park turn L, then R at Old Rectory and descend. Go L on to public footpath, go through gap stile, cross field and descend, keeping R. Cross bridge, go through gate then gap stile and follow waymarkers downhill, keeping stream and wood on your R.

❷ When wall heads L go through gap stile on your R continuing downhill into National Trust land at Ladyside. Cross stile, go through wood then leave it via another stile. Turn R, still continuing downhill to stile leading on to Manifold Way.

❸ Cross Manifold Way, then bridge and take path uphill following signs for Thor's Cave. Anyone who has seen Ken Russell's film, The Lair of the White Worm (1988), may feel slightly apprehensive when climbing up the hillside towards Thor's Cave. Fiction apart, Thor's Cave was formed over thousands of

years from the combined effecs of wind and rain on the soft limestone. Excavations have revealed it to be the site of a Bronze-Age burial. At mouth of cave turn L, continue on track uphill, curve right at stile and follow path to summit for views over Manifold Valley.

❹ Retrace your steps to Manifold Way and turn L. Continue past caravan park and then cross 2 bridges. At beginning of 3rd bridge cross stile on R and follow path back, parallel to road and then curving L and uphill.

❺ Go across stile by dried up pond and follow path uphill with wall on your R. Go through gap stile adjacent to barn. Keep on, go through next gap stile and church spire at Grindon should be visible ahead.

❻ Continue on this path across fields, cross stile, go through 4 gap stiles then turn L over final stile on to farm road. Follow this road, keeping on when it becomes lane then turn R on to road opposite Chestnut Cottage, take 1st L back to car park.

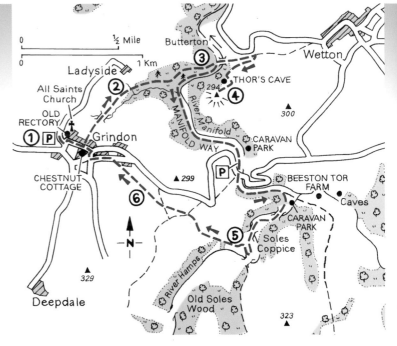

Apedale A Mining Tradition

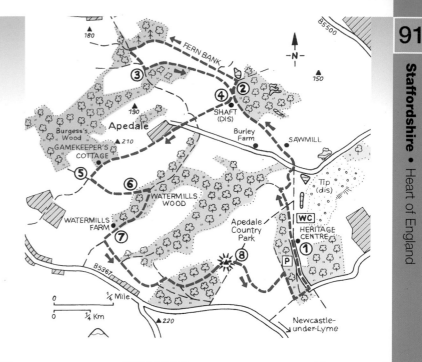

4¾ miles (7.7km) 2hrs **Ascent:** 300ft (91m)

Paths:	Wide gravel tracks, roads and dirt trails, 10 stiles
Suggested map:	OS Explorer 258 Stoke-on-Trent
Grid reference:	SJ 822483
Parking:	Ample parking opposite Heritage Centre

Exploring a wasteland returned to nature.

1 From **Heritage Centre** in **Apedale Country Park** take path to go **R**, through gate. After 400yds (366m) turn **R** down to corner of park, then continue straight ahead, passing to **L** of **sawmill**. At fork, head **R** down short hill to corner of lake.

2 Ignoring stile, turn **L** along narrow path into woods. Follow most obvious trail to emerge into Fern Bank, exotic landscape of giant ferns. Follow path to junction of many paths, with clearing to your **L**. Walk through clearing to main gravel track.

3 Turn **L** and continue for 600yds (549m) to gate and turn-off for lake (Point **2**). About 30 paces after gate, head **R** up signed footpath along edge of small copse, keeping fence to your **R**. At top of this wood, 30 paces off track to your **L**, is **disused mineshaft**.

4 From top of wood continue up tree-lined track to village of **Apedale**, former mining community. On **R**, just after track veers to **L**, is **Gamekeeper's Cottage**.

5 About 100yds (91m) beyond cottage turn **L** along track to gate; bear **L** after gate down well-trodden meadow path to stile. After stile, head **R** following fence to bottom of hill, then skirt **L** to stile.

6 Cross into **Watermills Wood** and follow trail to stile, then junction of 2 paths. Head **R** here and, after 10 paces, fork **R** again. Shortly you cross series of stiles before continuing up to **Watermills Farm**.

7 Go through gate and continue for 100yds (91m) before following footpath **L** over series of fields and stiles to farm buildings on your **R**. When fence veers round to **L**, follow it to edge of sapling plantation. At wide gravel track, head **R** and at fork go **L**. At next fork go **R** along tarmac to summit.

8 From summit drop down other side, continue over crossroads to pair of swing gates and T-junction. Head **R** here, and then take 1st **L** down hill. At tarmac road head **L** and continue back towards **Heritage Centre** and start.

Ilam The Compleat Angler

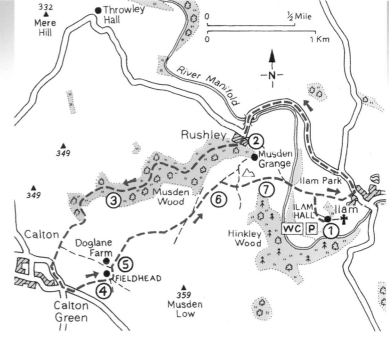

4¾ miles (7.7km) 2hrs 30min **Ascent:** 607ft (185m)

Paths:	Metalled roads, parkland, open hillside, meadows and forest tracks, boggy in wet weather
Suggested map:	OS Explorer OL24 White Peak
Grid reference:	SK 131507
Parking:	At Ilam Hall (National Trust)

Explore the countryside once walked by Izaak Walton, the 'Father of Angling'.

1 Exit car park from top, turn **R** then **R** again through gate; follow track through **park**. Cross stile and turn **L** on to road through **Ilam**. Go uphill, turn **L** at Park Cottage on to Castern to Throwley road. At Y-junction go **L**, following road across Rushley Bridge.

2 Go through Rushley Farm steading. Turn **R**, over ladder stile on to public footpath. Cross another ladder stile, walk along side of fence and cross gate on **L**. Continue following waymarked path beside stone wall and then fence. At next ladder stile keep ahead.

3 Go over another 4 stiles then, when you get to 5th, turn **L** on to road. At crossroads turn **L** towards Ashbourne. Go **L** through gap stile at next public footpath sign and cross field. Cross stile, go through another field to stile to **L** of farm then head diagonally **L** across next field.

4 Cross wall by stone steps, head diagonally **R** to gap stile to **R** of some buildings. Continue on this line to another stile in hedge to **R** of **Fieldhead** farm and turn **l** on to road. Follow this round boundary of farm and go over stile on **R**.

5 Follow well-defined path uphill past derelict building. Cross stile, cross field to where 2 walls meet at corner and follow wall to **R**. Join farm road, pass derelict steading, then turn diagonally **R** across field and through gap stile at far corner.

6 Follow direction pointer past 2 marker stones to next public footpath sign. Go **R**, through gap in wall and follow sign for **Ilam**. Follow wall on your **R**, go through gap, follow waymarker downhill, through gap stile and into **park**. Continue downhill and through another gap stile.

7 Go across field, stile then bridge and another stile, cross path and head uphill to **L** of path. At top of hill turn **R**, cross to caravan park and retrace your steps to car park.

93 Caldonlow Peak Geology

6 miles (9.7km) 2hrs 30min Ascent: 480ft (146m)
Paths: Gravel tracks, grassy trails and roads, 5 stiles
Suggested map: OS Explorer 259 Derby; OL24 White Peak
Grid reference: SK 086493 (on Explorer 259)
Parking: Ample parking at start point

The geology of this region provides a backdrop to a spectacular walk.

❶ From road corner head east along gravel track, walking away from **Cauldon**. Go through gate and continue up small valley. Pass barn on your R and go through slot or swing gate then take **R** fork along wide dirt track. At another gate ahead go **R** through gate then follow field round to **L**. After 30 paces go through gap in dry-stone wall and carry on straight up hill.

❷ At top **R-H** corner of field go through gate and head across next field to gap in dry-stone wall ahead. Head for bottom **L-H** corner of next field and cross stile on to A52. Bear **L** for 100yds (91m) then turn **R** along narrow metalled road up to **Weaver Farm**. As road veers **L** there are 2 footpath signs on **R**: at 1st of these go back on yourself, up hill towards gate in dry-stone wall.

❸ After crossing stile here keep following dry-stone wall to your R and at next gate continue in same

direction, with wall to your L. At end of this wall bear slightly **R** to join another wall on R and follow it to gate.

❹ Before crossing dry-stone wall ahead of you, go **L** for 100yds (91m) and then **R** over stile, before making straight for **trig point**. From trig point retrace your steps to stile, but instead of crossing it, head **L** across field, making for dry-stone wall at bottom. Follow this wall to **Wardlow**.

❺ Continue to **A52** and go straight across, following public footpath sign. Continue over thistly plateau of this field to stile. Across stile head straight through next field, making for **L-H** corner.

❻ Go **R** along base of field. Continue to bottom of hill and then bear slightly **L**, heading up and then downhill through succession of fields with trees to your L. At far end of fields, turn **L** for some 100yds (91m) and then **R** along trail through narrow valley. At bottom of valley rejoin main track to retrace your steps to start.

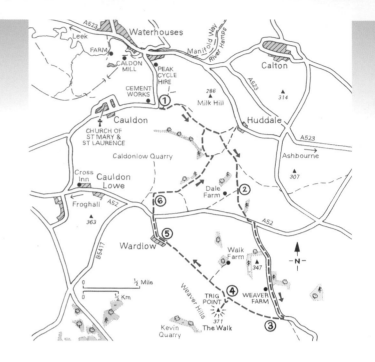

94 Ellastone A Fictional Past

3½ miles (5.7km) 1hr 30min Ascent: 360ft (110m)
Paths: Gravel tracks, roads and grass trails, 11 stiles
Suggested map: OS Explorer 259 Derby
Grid reference: SK 118426
Parking: Ample parking along roads

Discover the area that was the source of inspiration for author George Eliot and composer George Handel.

❶ Ellastone, the start of the walk, inspired the setting of *Adam Bede*. From **post office** go **L** and then take 1st **L** down obvious gravel track. At junction of 2 bridleways, keep going straight to **Calwich Abbey**, where Handel composed *The Messiah* while staying with friends. Follow track **L** of abbey and along metalled road as far as **Calwich Home Farm**.

❷ Pass farm and follow track round to **L** of **The Grove** and through gate. At fork follow yellow footpath arrows to your **L** and, after 50yds (46m), veer **L** off track up short hill to stile in front of **Cockley** farm. Cross stile and head just to **R** of **Cockley**, following dirt and grass track all way to B5032.

❸ At road go **L** and then 1st **R**, through **Calwichbank Farm** and up gravel track. When track bears round to R, keep going straight into field,

making for gap in hedge at top **R-H** corner. Shortly after this gap, go through gate on **R** and then follow hedge **L**, down field.

❹ At bottom follow hedge round to **L** and cut diagonally **R** across field to stile. After crossing stile, skirt round top of wood to another stile and continue as far as **Hutts Farm**. After stile take gravel track up hill to gate into farmyard and head straight on to another stile into field.

❺ Continue straight across this field making for corner of **Aldercarr Wood**. Keep going to stile in bottom **R-H** corner of field and carry on along **R-H** edge of next field. At far end is another stile, cross this and continue straight to B5032. Turn **R** along road and, after 100yds (91m), take path to **L**. Head diagonally **R** across field to double stile and then **L** round bottom of small mound with trees. Keep going as far as junction of 2 bridleways, at Point ❶, and from here retrace your steps back to post office.

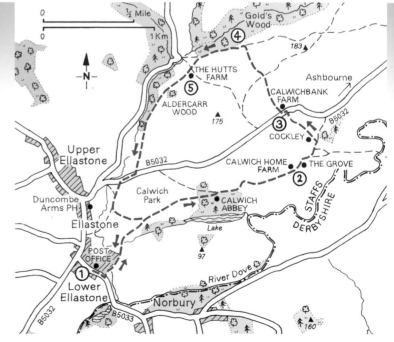

Barlaston In Wedgwood Country

3¼ miles (5.3km) 1hr 15min Ascent: 180ft (55m) ▲

Paths: Roads, gravel tracks and tow paths, 1 stile
Suggested map: OS Explorer 258 Stoke-on-Trent
Grid reference: SJ 889395
Parking: Ample parking along road at starting point

A gentle, short walk exploring the life and times of the Staffordshire Potteries' most famous son, Josiah Wedgwood.

❶ From **visitors' centre** drive head **L** across river and then **R** up drive towards **Barlaston Hall**. Go past this hall and continue along metalled road as far as crossroads in **Barlaston**. Josiah set up his first pottery factory in Burslem in 1759 and revolutionised what up until that point had been a cottage industry. Rather than rely on family members he paid people to work in the factory. A decade later and with business booming Josiah built a bigger factory in Burslem and this became a model for other pottery manufacturers. At crossroads turn **R** and after 250yds (229m), just past St John's Church on your **L**, head **L** along wide gravel track. This track passes through broad expanse of open farmland, with sweeping (if not altogether dramatic) views of Trent and Mersey canal to **R** and, beyond, flood plain of Trent Valley.

❷ After about 800yds (732m), you get to gate ahead of you: from here follow less obvious track **R**, around to stile where another track comes in on **L**. After crossing stile head **R** along track, straight over railway, before bearing **R** to bridge over canal. Go over bridge and take steps down to **L**.

❸ At bottom of steps head **L** and then follow canal all way to 1st bridge (at Barlaston) and then 2nd (at Wedgwood Station). The **Trent and Mersey Canal**, completed in 1777, linked the River Trent at Derwent Mouth near Derby with the Bridgewater Canal at Preston Brook, near the mouth of the Mersey. This effectively meant that the country could be navigated all the way from the west coast to the east and that fine clay from the West Country could be shipped to the doorstep of Josiah Wedgwood's factories. Head **L** here, up to metalled road, and then **R**, back towards visitors' centre. To find out more about Wedgwood, visit The Wedgwood Story **visitors' centre**.

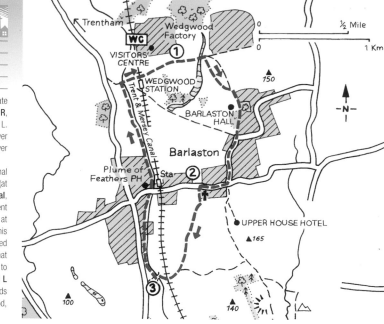

Hanbury The Crater

4¼ miles (6.8km) 2hrs Ascent: 240ft (73m) ▲

Paths: Meadow tracks and bridleways, 27 stiles
Suggested map: OS Explorer 245 The National Forest
Grid reference: SK 170279
Parking: St Werburgh's Church car park

The site of the biggest non-nuclear explosion of World War II.

❶ From car park, go back along Church Lane and after 150yds (137m), go **R** through car park and over stile. Cross field to pair of stiles over road and continue across field to gate, then to corner of hedge With hedge to your **R**, head for **Knightsfield Farm**.

❷ Go through farm courtyard and along rough surfaced track. As it bears **R**, follow footpath sign, **L**, across stiles, keeping hedge to L. At turning circle, go across to stile and footbridge before continuing, with hedge to L, to stile before road.

❸ Turn **R**, then 1st **L** before **Crown Inn**, across car park. Cross into field ahead to stile at bottom. Continue up next field, crossing stile under tree at top.

❹ Where hedge goes **L**, follow it across stile and aim for far **R** of **Hanbury Park**. In top **R-H** corner of field, go through gate to road. Turn **L**, going through gate into farm courtyard, then through gate to **R**.

Continue on bridleway to **Woodend**.

❺ At road head **R** for 100yds (91m) then **L** through gate, to stile in fence to **R**. Head diagonally **L** across field to stile, continue across next field to stile. Cross **Capertition Wood** to open field, continuing with hedge to L, up hill, across stile, then down to stile. At end of field go through gate.

❻ Skirting to **L** of **farm**, climb over succession of stiles before turning **L** through iron gate. Head across field keeping hedge to L. At end cross stile on **L** and go **R** towards **R-H** end of trees.

❼ Head **R** up short hill to stile, continue to stile amongst trees. Head round to **L** to **crater**. Follow path round to **L**, past **memorial** stone, to bridleway leading away.

❽ At end of bridleway head **L** across field, keeping hedge to R. Go through gap in hedge ahead and continue ahead to gate at top. At end of hedge on **L** go through gate and stile to return to **Hanbury**.

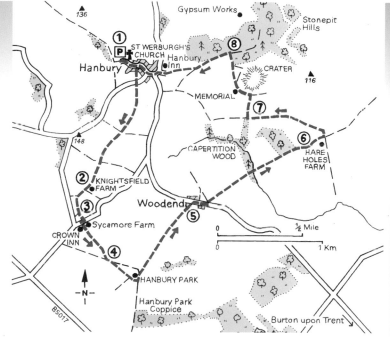

97 Shugborough Through the Estate

4¾ miles (7.7km) 2hrs **Ascent:** 180ft (55m) ⚠

Paths: Gravel tracks, roads and tow paths
Suggested map: OS Explorer 244 Cannock Chase
Grid reference: SK 004205
Parking: Ample parking at start point

To Staffordshire's greatest country house.

❶ Take **R-H** path at end of Seven Springs car park and continue **R** at fork shortly after. Follow wide gravel track, ignoring all paths to L or R, and continue as far as **Stepping Stones**. Ford stream here and head **R** as far as major T-junction.

❷ Head **R** here, following **Staffordshire Way** footpath sign. Continue along wide gravel track, again ignoring less obvious paths to L or R, as far as A513. Cross road carefully and follow it **R** for 400yds (366m) before turning **L**, again following **Staffordshire Way** footpath signs.

❸ Follow metalled road past **Staffordshire County Museum** and **Shugborough Park Farm**. Shortly after Park Farm, continue along Staffordshire Way, ignoring more direct path L to house itself. Follow bridleway all way to **Essex Bridge**. If you do want closer look at façade, head **L** instead and follow path round past front of house; it's signed as private drive but this is

meant more for cars, and it is open to public when grounds are open. If you continue all way round you'll eventually rejoin main route just before **Essex Bridge**. From close range it's also interesting to note that the columns aren't made of stone at all, but wood that has been clad with slate and painted to look like stone, a solution that would have been considerably cheaper.

❹ By way of short diversion, just 350yds (320m) to north of **Essex Bridge**, heading **L** along tow path, is junction of Trent and Mersey and Staffordshire and Worcestershire canals. Toll-keeper's cottage has disappeared, but toll-house with arched windows and kiosk still remain on south side of latter. Go across bridge and head **R** along canal (cross **Essex Bridge** and canal to reach Lockhouse Restaurant on L). Follow tow path for 1 mile (1.6km) and, at **Navigation Farm**, head **R** on metalled road. Carry on over **Weetman's Bridge**, cross **A513** carefully, and continue up short drive back to car park.

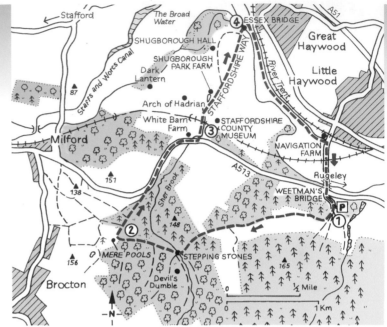

98 Cannock Chase Memorials to the Brave

4 miles (6.4km) 1hr 30min **Ascent:** 361ft (110m) ⚠

Paths: Gravel tracks and roads
Suggested map: OS Explorer 244 Cannock Chase
Grid reference: SK 980181
Parking: Ample parking at start point
Note: Beware of cyclists

This heathland walk around the wartime cemeteries serves as a poignant reminder of less peaceful times.

❶ From **Glacial Boulder**, walk away from road along narrow dirt trail for about 40 paces and then turn **R** along wide gravel track. When you get to fork, go **R**, following **Heart of England Way** footpath sign.

❷ At next major fork, continue in same direction (ignoring footpath off to R). At next path crossroads, again carry straight on as path curves gradually around to **R**. Continue along this track across 2 more path crossroads until your path curves round to **L** alongside road. At point where another wide track comes in from L, go straight on rather than taking shortcut down to road.

❸ After crossing narrow surfaced road opposite **Springslade Lodge**, continue up dirt track and across path crossroads. After about 500yds (457m) you

come to T-junction in path that requires dog-leg **R** then **L** to keep going in same direction through car park. Continue in this direction to 2nd car park and, as track curves around to **L**, another metalled road.

❹ Turn **L** past **German War Cemetery** until road becomes wide gravel track. Continue along this track, down into woods, and when you get to fork go **L** down hill, ignoring path heading uphill to R.

❺ Continue along bottom of valley for 1 mile (1.6km), staying to **R** of stream, until you get to obvious ford. Cross stream using stepping stones. At junction on other side head away from stream following track **L** around bottom of hill ahead, rather than R, straight over top of it. Follow this track as it curves round to **R**, all way to top of hill.

❻ Continue across plateau until path starts to descend other side, at which point you rejoin path, heading **R**, back towards start and car park.

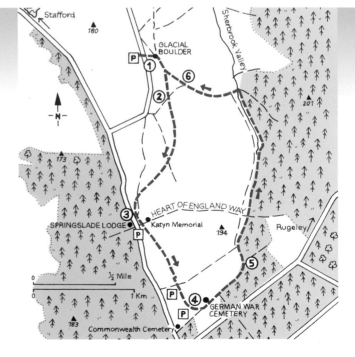

Lichfield Soaring Heaven on Earth

2½ miles (4km) 1hr **Ascent:** Negligible

Paths: Roads, surfaced paths and dirt trails
Suggested map: OS Explorers 232 Nuneaton & Tamworth; 244 Cannock Chase
Grid reference: SK 118095 (on Explorer 232)
Parking: Ample paid parking in Lichfield town centre

A town walk and a magnificent cathedral.

❶ From **tourist information centre** head **R** along Bore Street and then **L** along Conduit Street, leading to Market Square. Pass Market Square on your **L** and carry straight along Dam Street, past tea shops and cafés, until you get to Pool Walk. Go **L** here, keeping pool on your R-H side, until you get to Beacon Street.

❷ Go diagonally **R** over Beacon Street to public toilets and entrance to park. Skirt around **L-H** edge of park, keeping first bowling lawn and then tennis courts to your **R**. After tennis courts follow path round to **R** and, at next path junction, walk **L**, continuing around edge of park.

❸ At car park bear slightly **R**, following path to far end of playing fields. After path has entered narrow band of trees, and just before **A51**, turn **R** along narrow dirt trail and carry on to **golf course**. Just before golf course, turn **R** and follow small brook back along edge of playing fields to little duck pond.

(Canoes for hire in summer.) Continue on past pond before crossing over footbridge to **L** to Shaw Lane.

❹ Follow Shaw Lane to **Beacon Street**, then go **R** for 150yds (137m) and then **L** along The Close to cathedral. If you're not in any rush, visit cathedral before continuing. There's an excellent shop with leaflets and guides and free leaflet is also available, which describes the cathedral's highlights. Bear to **R** of cathedral and, at end of The Close, just after Cathedral Coffee Shop, go **R** down Dam Street and then immediately **L** along footpath to **Stowe Pool**. From far end of Stowe Pool you can look back at cathedral's towers and see through windows from one side to the other, giving the impression that they're lighter and more delicate than stone.

❺ When path divides into 2 parallel tracks, follow cycle path sign. Continue around pool and back to Dam Street, before retracing your steps to tourist information centre at start.

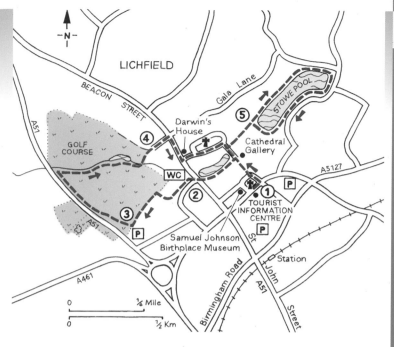

Trysull Wine-lover's Delight

5¼ miles (8.4km) 1hr 45min **Ascent:** 270ft (82m)

Paths: Roads, grass and dirt trails, gravel tracks, 3 stiles
Suggested map: OS Explorer 219 Wolverhampton & Dudley
Grid reference: SJ 852942
Parking: Ample street parking in Trysull

An escarpment walk taking in a vineyard.

❶ From **All Saints' Church**, head north along **Trysull Holloway** for 100yds (91m) and, after crossing small brook, go **L** along **Church Lane** as far as **Seisdon** (this might be muddy after heavy rain, so suitable footwear is recommended). Turn **L** on to road (there is no pavement here, so exercise caution) and then take first **R** towards **Lea Farm**.

❷ Follow this road to T-junction with **Fox Road**, heading **L** then immediately **R** towards **Woodcote**. Stay on this track round to **R**, following signs for **Staffordshire Way** and, at top of lane, go through swing gate to continue along narrower dirt trail. At corner of hedge follow path **L** around edge of field and then immediately **R** up to Wolmore Lane.

❸ Head **L** along this metalled road and then **R** along **Tinker's Castle Road**. At top of hill, just before **cottage** on **L**, head **L** up path between wall and fence. Continue along edge of escarpment for 1¼ miles

(2km), until it joins B4176. Just after junction, head **R** along track down to **vineyard**. To continue from here, keep going along B4176 for 50yds (46m), and turn off **L** over stile (there's no pavement, but plenty of grass on L-H side of road).

❹ Go across middle of field to stile then follow hedge just to your **R** in same direction. At far R-H corner of this field keep ahead, aiming for tree in hedge ahead. Go through wide gap in hedge and bear slightly **L** to cross this next field all way to **Crockington Lane**. (If this field is impassable because of crops, it may be easier to bear **R** along hedge to **Fiershill Farm**, but this means longer walk along road into Trysull.)

❺ Cross stile to Crockington Lane then go **R** for 100yds (91m), before turning **L** through kissing gate. Go straight on across this field to another gate and then down track between houses to **Seisdon Road**. Turn **R** here, back to start.

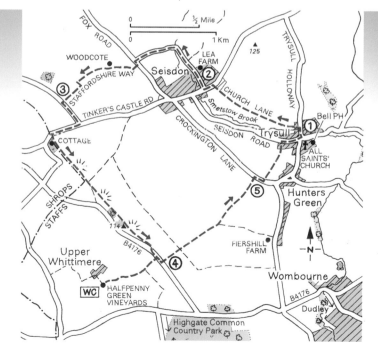

Walking in Safety

All these walks are suitable for any reasonably fit person, but less experienced walkers should try the easier walks first. Route finding is usually straightforward, but you will find that an Ordnance Survey map is a useful addition to the route maps and descriptions.

Risks

Although each walk has been researched with a view to minimising the risks to the walkers who follow its route, no walk in the countryside can be considered to be completely free from risk. Walking in the outdoors will always require a degree of common sense and judgement to ensure that it is as safe as possible.

- Be particularly careful on cliff paths and in upland terrain, where the consequences of a slip can be very serious.

- Remember to check tidal conditions before walking along the seashore.

- Some sections of route are by, or cross roads. Take care and remember traffic is a danger even on minor country lanes.

- Be careful around farmyard machinery and livestock, especially if you have children or a dog with you.

- Be aware of the consequences of changes of weather and check the forecast before you set off. Carry spare clothing and a torch if you are walking in the winter months. Remember that the weather can change very quickly at any time of the year, and in moorland and heathland areas, mist and fog can make route finding much harder. Don't set out in these conditions unless you are confident of your navigation skills in poor visibility. In summer remember to take account of the heat and sun; wear a hat and carry spare water.

- On walks away from centres of population you should carry a whistle and survival bag. If you do have an accident requiring the emergency services, make a note of your position as accurately as possible and dial 999.

Equipment

- The most important single item of equipment for country walking is a good pair of sturdy boots or walking shoes. Boots give better support to your ankles, especially in rough or hill country, and your feet need to be kept warm and dry in all conditions.

- Britain's climate is unpredictable, so warm and waterproof clothing is the next essential, but you don't need to spend a fortune on an Everest-specification jacket for a gentle stroll. There are many efficient and breathable alternatives which need not cost the earth. Waterproof trousers or gaiters are also a good idea and, as up to 40 per cent of body heat is lost through the head, a warm hat is essential.

- None of the walks in this book will take more than a day, but you will need a rucksack to hold extra clothing, food and drink for the longer walks. Look for one with about a 20 to 35-litre capacity, with stormproof pockets for your map, compass (a good ideal on any hill walk), camera and other bits and pieces.